The
Last
Victim

*The case that ended
30 years of sexual deviance*

**By CHRISTOPHER RUDY
with
GEORGE DAVIS**

ISBN – 13:978-1468017601
ISBN – 10: 1468017608
LCCN: 2011962099

Printed by CreateSpace
In North Charleston, SC

Author: Christopher Rudy
with George Davis

Our thanks to those who granted permission for quotes in their publications to be used at the top of each chapter in
The Last Victim.

Six of the quotes are reprinted with permission of the
Akron Beacon Journal and Ohio.com

One quote was reprinted with permission
of the Canton Repository

Quote reprinted with permission from *Virgin or Vamp: How the Press Covers Sex Crimes* by Helen Benedict, Oxford University Press, 1992

Our thanks also to:
Book Interior and Cover Designer Li Hertzi
of Li Hertzi Design of Canton Ohio
And
Website Designer Jennifer C. McInnis
Charleston, S.C.
www.thelastvictim.net

Authors' Note

To protect the identities of victims and their families plus others who have requested anonymity, fictitious names will be noted in *italic* type the first time each appears.

Dedicated to our wives,

KIM and MERLEEN, for their

patience and understanding,

and all the law enforcement

personnel whose lives were

touched in any way by

The Ski-Mask Rapist

A special thanks to the members
of the Stark County Crime Lab.
Without their diligence, none
of this would have been possible.

"Rapists are about the lowest of the low. They victimize people who aren't in a position to defend them.
The crime is so heinous that it affects not just the victim but the whole community at large."

-- *Philip W. Paar, former Jackson Township, Ohio, police chief*

Chapter 1

Despicable!

This single word perfectly describes the ski-mask rapist accused of preying on females across Ohio, Michigan and Arizona over three decades before being convicted of only two Northeast Ohio sexual assaults out of 60 suspected cases.

This life-threatening sexual deviate, whose life is chronicled on the following pages, lurked in bushes right outside homes and apartments, watching mothers and daughters in various stages of undress before turning from "peeping" into knife-point rapes combined with threats of death unless the victims cooperated.

Under the cover of darkness, primarily in the home county of the Pro Football Hall of Fame in Canton, Ohio, William E. Griffith Jr. perpetrated his evil deeds. He used the nighttime as his cover as he crept behind bushes and breathed through a dark-colored ski mask to take what he wanted from countless, unsuspecting women, who were enveloped in a feeling of security while in their own homes.

The one place in our homes where many feel most secure is the bedroom. Occupants feel safe and secure once they have locked the doors, turned off the lights and tucked the kids in for the evening, then crawled into bed themselves and went to sleep. However, it was in the bedroom where evil entered countless women's lives as they slept under the blanket of darkness. Evil stole from these victims the most personal gift they had to give another human being: themselves. Evil took them by force, wearing a ski mask and gloves while clutching a knife and flashlight.

Based on many years of investigation and information from across the country, we know William E. Griffith Jr. stood in the bushes of scores of houses across Northeast Ohio. In the late 1970's he was content to watch through the windows at countless victims and pleasure himself. After a few years, Griffith apparently tired of merely watching and underwent a metamorphosis: He crossed the thresholds of women's residences and raped his targeted prey. Mere peeping no longer quieted the urge inside him.

Griffith's spree of voyeurism arrests and attacks on women as they slept comfortably in their beds, only to be awakened by a gloved hand placed over their mouths and a bright flashlight beam shining in their eyes, covered three decades. The victims were all told the same thing: "I'm just going to take a few things. I won't hurt you. . . . Get up and come with me. . . " The monster then would order his victims to disrobe. He would shine his light up and down their bodies before ordering them to lie down. Then the sex acts he desired began.

When retired Jackson Township, Ohio, Police Lt. Christopher Rudy attended the March 2009 "Victim Impact" portion of the parole hearing process for William E. Griffith Jr., the detective sat in awe as he listened to *Melissa Brown* speak about the attack she had endured more than two decades earlier.

As the hearing continued, the Ohio Parole Board hearing officer, *Molly Scott,* stopped Melissa. She asked, "I'm sorry, but I can't keep the victims straight in this case, Melissa. Which one are you?" Brown responded, "I'm the one whose case put him in prison." Scott responded, "Oh, OK. You're the last one; you're the last victim." At that moment, Rudy had an epiphany. What a great title for a book! Several days later, Rudy phoned old friend George Davis, a retired investigative crime reporter, with the idea of writing a book about Griffith's 30-year saga of criminal sexual conduct.

This book contains information developed from interviews with more than two dozen people who had a part in the investigation that eventually led to William E. Griffith Jr.'s conviction. There also are highlights from conversations with his three former wives.

This book chronicles Griffith's voyeurism and rape activities from the late 1950s as a teenager to his time in the U.S. Army and his post-discharge relocation to Michigan with his young bride, *Teresa Martin,* the first of his three wives, to his attacks in Northeast Ohio and his subsequent arrest and conviction. Griffith was a smooth-talking salesman, who led law enforcement around the country on a manhunt that criss-crossed Ohio, Michigan, Minnesota, Oklahoma and ultimately ended in Phoenix, Arizona.

The case against Griffith is unique in the annals of Stark County criminal justice since it was the first DNA case in the county's rich history of criminal activity. In our memory, there has never been another criminal whose activities devastated so many women, families and friends as William E. Griffith Jr.'s reign of terror wrought.

When one considers the most notorious criminals in the history of Northeast Ohio, murderers or deadly arsonists are usually considered. We contend that William E. Griffith Jr. is a serial rapist whose life of voyeurism and rape impacted hundreds of lives from 1958 until his last known rape in 1988. At least 60 sexual crimes have been attributed to him, though he was convicted of only two rapes and three misdemeanor voyeurism charges in Ohio and Michigan.

What makes this story so troubling is the belief of many that had current technology been available in the early days of this hideous saga, many of the rapes might never have occurred. The rapist likely would have been caught through DNA, forensics, or the now widely used Automated Fingerprint Identification System (AFIS). The latter system takes unknown latent fingerprints from a crime scene and automatically seeks to match them with prints from a known offender. During the time of this crime spree, an investigator had to have a known suspect for fingerprint comparison. AFIS came into use a few years after Griffith's capture.

Since Griffith's prison incarceration in December 1988, he was convicted in neighboring Portage County, Ohio, for raping a 17-year-old girl. Portage County sheriff's investigators had submitted a rape kit[1] to the FBI that positively identified Griffith as her attacker.

Born in November 1942 and an Ohio prison inmate for 23 years, Griffith has sought parole without success. According to Ohio prison records, Griffith earned an associate's degree in human services and a bachelor's degree in sociology and psychology while incarcerated. Ohio Department of Rehabilitation and Correction records show he will not be eligible for parole again until 2019.

The twists and turns that led to Griffith's unmasking, capture and conviction are haunting and remarkable, according to his chief nemesis, Christopher Rudy, as told to long-time investigative reporter and author George Davis.

---

1 A rape kit is a term used by professionals in both medical and criminal justice communities to describe forensic trace evidence collected from the body of a victim, male or female. It contains fingernail scrapings, as well as vaginal, oral and anal swabs.

…"There are no words to describe what I
experienced on April 12, 1988"…

Melissa Brown, rape victim, addressing the Stark County Court
Akron Beacon Journal, December 17, 1988

Chapter 2

What many have called the beginning of the end for William E. Griffith Jr. came on the quiet, dark, early morning of April 12, 1988, less than two weeks after April Fool's Day. What happened to Melissa Brown, 24, in the wee hours of April 12th was anything but a belated April Fool's joke. It was for real. And the single mother, then living in a Jackson Township duplex, remembers the events as if they occurred yesterday.

Still a resident of Northeast Ohio, Melissa's sexual assault was the eighth reported rape in the Jackson area over an eight-year period and, according to my investigation, Griffith's last known rape in Jackson Township.

Speaking on condition her true identity would not be used, Melissa said she felt safe at home and at work – despite the rapes that had been reported in the area but never revealed to her by her rental company. She was sexually assaulted on her living-room floor as her son, 3, slept in his nearby bedroom. The rapist followed his historic pattern, removing and mangling the window screen and throwing it on the roof to permit him access to his prey.

"I know he must have gotten in my house that way because this was early April and the windows were closed and locked. He unlocked the window after he had cut the screen and raised the window to get inside," Melissa said.

The woman said of her attacker, "He stunk like oil and grease. I couldn't see his face or hands because he wore a ski mask and gloves. However, I was able to catch glimpses of his white skin. To be honest, he didn't hurt me physically, just emotionally, but he scarred me for the rest of my life."

The odor of grease and oil from that night of terror still haunts her now more than 20 years later. "I often become nauseated at the slightest smell of oil or grease and I suffer flashbacks to that horrific night," Melissa said.

The flashbacks always seem to occur when she has her oil changed or when she finds herself at a mechanic's garage. "The dreaded attack comes right back every time," she said. It is true that smells take people back to specific incidents in their lives. It is one of the things that make her attack so tragic.

Melissa lived in the Jackson duplex only six months before the rape occurred. She never lived there after the attack. She moved in with her parents for awhile before living alone again with her young son.

Recounting for me the details of that fateful morning, Melissa said she had been home all evening following work. She and her son had been sleeping when the attack occurred about 3 a.m.

"I thought I had heard someone in the house minutes before he was in my room, but I thought if I acted like I was asleep he would take what he wanted and leave. I heard the front door open and close, so I reached over and picked up the phone to call police but the line was dead. In a moment there was a bright beam of light shining in on me through my bedroom window. I closed my eyes and faked like I was sleeping.

"The next thing I heard was someone coming in the front door again and I saw a beam of light coming up my hallway. I was petrified and startled by my attacker's hand over my mouth and a knife against my throat. He told me to do what he said and I wouldn't get hurt. I followed his orders, hoping he would be gone in a matter of minutes without hurting me or *Johnny*."

"He prefaced every command to me with the word 'fuck.' After his initial words, he told me to get fucking out of bed, go into the fucking living room and get down on the floor on my fucking back. He handed me a pillow, and said to put the pillow over my fucking face. The entire time I was just thinking, 'If I cooperate, he'll do what he wants to do and then get out.'

"He asked me if I wanted to do oral or vaginal sex and I told him to please not make me do oral, so he didn't. When my son cried, he let me go check on him and then return to the living room. He told me to play with him and get him excited; he had a difficult time maintaining any kind of erection. He must have gotten Vaseline out of my bathroom medicine cabinet prior to getting me out of my room, because I noticed the jar on the living-room floor when I returned. He put it on me and penetrated me."

"Then he started asking me questions about my life. When he asked if I was practicing birth control, I replied 'no' and he immediately stopped the assault. He then told me to go to my son's bedroom and remain there for a half hour. He also warned me not to call the police. He said he lived in the neighborhood, and if he saw a cruiser around my house during the next week he'd come back and do me again."

(The statement about living in the neighborhood turned out to be bogus once police targeted Griffith as the rapist. Investigators knew Griffith was living in Hartville, about 10 miles northeast of Melissa's duplex.)

Melissa waited about 20 minutes before trying to call police, only to discover that the phones were still dead as her attacker had cut the lines outside. He also tossed a cordless receiver on the roof as he exited. The phone was found in the rain gutter.

Knowing she had to take action to protect herself and her son, Melissa ran to her neighbor's portion of the duplex and called police, while the male occupant ran to her residence and rescued the child.

She said the house was dark throughout the encounter, but she could see that he was a white man because of the skin color between his coat sleeve and glove. She also noted that he wore a ski mask to hide his identity – the same method of operation used in other rape cases attributed to Griffith but not prosecuted because the then six-year statute of limitations had expired. The statute of limitations for sexual assault in Ohio was not changed until 2000 when the state legislature extended the time limitation to 20 years.

Asked what she would do differently if the attack occurred now, Melissa responded defiantly, "I would have fought like hell. I'm a strong person, but back then I wasn't and I feared for my son, who the rapist threatened to kill along with me if I didn't do what he said."

Melissa was told there would be several victims testifying, but when trial was just days away she learned that she would be the only person to testify because the evidence was strongest in her case and because of the statute of limitations. "When I learned that, I kept telling myself, 'I don't know if I can do this. I don't know if I can do this.'

"I was prepped for testimony by an assistant Stark County prosecutor, and then we learned that the trial was being cancelled because he (Griffith) had agreed to plead guilty. I was given the opportunity prior to his sentencing to make an impact statement and he was then taken to prison.

Hopefully, I and the other victims will never have to see him again."

In 2009, she testified at the victim impact portion of Griffith's parole hearing. Griffith was not present.

Her wish for her attacker is clear and understandable: "I hope that he never walks out of prison, considering all the lives he has ruined and/or changed. He's where he deserves to be," she told me after the parole hearing.

Melissa still finds it difficult to be at a mall or at any public place now that she has seen her rapist's photo and seen him in court. "I am constantly checking out my surroundings wherever I'm at, and once in a while I'll stop dead in my tracks because I see someone who looks like him. Then I realize he's still in prison and I am safe."

Since she was raped, Melissa has been married and divorced twice. She had not been devoutly religious until the past 12 years, but now attends church regularly. Her two children and her job are her life now.

"I still haven't found Mr. Right," she said. Her son, now 26, was never told of the rape until he reached adulthood. Now a teenager, her daughter still does not know about the abuse, fear and agony that her mother had to endure long before she was conceived.

..."*Dad was always a good provider and
father but he has a Jekyll-and-Hyde personality*"...

Robert Griffith, Akron Beacon Journal, August 1988

Chapter 3

World War II embodied the best of times and the worst
of times; the best of the human race, and the most maniacal
and inhumane. Across the Atlantic in 1942, Germany's
Adolph Hitler had his plan for world domination on full
display. On November 6th that year, headlines in the *Akron
(Ohio) Beacon Journal* trumpeted the success of British Lt. Gen.
Bernard L. Montgomery in driving wedges through the Axis
lines commanded by German Field Marshal Erwin Rommel
and pushing the Germans and Italians into Libya and Egypt
while capturing 13,000 enemy soldiers.

In Akron, it was cold and rainy that Friday, with a high
temperature of 38 degrees. William E. Griffith Sr., a 20-year-
old dual-saw operator at Aircraft Corporation in Akron, and
his young bride, Maudie Mae (Meese) Griffith, 19, of New
Philadelphia, were at People's Hospital (later known as Akron
General Medical Center) celebrating the birth of son William
Edward Griffith Jr. at 9:18 that morning. After a short hospital
stay, they took their son home to 1504 Hampton Road in
Akron.

The Griffiths tried over the years for more children,
succeeding only once more – 10 years later. As the years
rolled by and William Jr. (Bill) grew up, the family rented
different houses around Akron and enrolled their son in the
Akron public schools. Bill first attended Crouse Elementary
and then Margaret Park Elementary when the family moved
to Central Akron. On February 26, 1951, William Sr. was

hired at the 7 Up Bottling Co. in Flint, Michigan, and moved his young family north. Four years later, they returned to Akron on Seward Avenue after William Sr. got another job. Bill attended Perkins Junior High School until 1957 when he entered Buchtel High School and the family moved to Storer Avenue. Bill took summer classes in 1961 in order to graduate. His GPA at graduation was 1.1. Bill would later state he was disinterested and unmotivated in high school. He claimed he was just glad to get out.

During his senior year, according to the high school yearbook, Bill was on the Farewell Committee. His preferences were listed as: Fast, blue '59 Impalas, Family, Lynn, and Police Car 9. No one knows what the reference to Police Car 9 meant. Also listed was William's high school nickname, "Stroker." While I believe "Stroker" referred to "stroker kits" for car engines to improve their "muscle" and RPMs (revolutions per minute), that nickname held a disturbing dual meaning in light of subsequent events.

Bill recalled his family was like other American families in the 1950s. I learned Bill was afraid of his father while growing up due to his dad's heavy drinking. His mother did not drink a lot, but at times she did imbibe. Bill's father was not an emotional man; his mother was "distant" emotionally. Griffith later pointed out that he got his share of spankings, but added he didn't feel there was any sexual inappropriateness in his rearing.

As the youngster was growing up, the family had a lot of parties, with drinking being the focal point. Bill believed his father had multiple affairs, and his mother accused her husband of that many times after finding lipstick on his handkerchief.

Mom worked full time at a local grocery store. Reflecting back on his childhood and his mother working outside the home, Bill remembered having rheumatic fever and his mother still going to work, leaving him alone. He figured he was then 8 years old. Despite such incidents, he said he felt loved and that his parents were protective of him. At the same time they trusted him to make good choices, and let him pretty much do what he wanted.

Bill felt he got along best with his grandmother on his father's side. He remembers her scolding him constantly for sliding down the banister at home because, as he put it, he "liked how it felt." His mother and grandmother told him what he was doing was wrong.

He remembered exploring his sexuality at age 8 while at a sleep-over and awakened to discover his friend between his legs playing with his private parts. Again, at 17 Bill had a sexual encounter with a different male. Bill began looking in other people's windows at around age 16, which is about the time he developed a habit of masturbation.

Based on our research and interviews, Bill's addiction with masturbation and voyeurism manifested itself in the United States Army. Bill stood outside the windows of homes while watching women and fantasizing about them as he masturbated and sometimes fell asleep in the process. Bill's lack of sleep and rest caused him to be late for work in the Army, which resulted in discipline. Bill revealed at its worst that his addiction to masturbation reached a high of 30 times a day.

Bill always took jobs that enabled his addiction. He was good at sales and was out on the road where he could search for potential targets.

"These people have no intention of following the rules and even when they register police can't just kick them out of the community...so it's important that everybody pay attention to their surroundings. Sex offenders don't look much different from anyone else."

Paul Rogers, American Lawyer and politician, 1921-2008

Chapter 4

Teresa Martin graduated from high school in Wayne, Michigan, in 1962. During an interview, she told me, "I always wanted to be in the medical field and, in particular, I wanted to be an X-ray technician. The U.S. Army gave me the best opportunity to reach my goal. I got the training for being an X-ray tech, but I'll tell you what, going into the Army sure made me grow up in a hurry."

In January 1963, Teresa did her training at Fort Sam Houston in Texas. That's where she met William E. Griffith Jr., who was training to become a lab technician. Teresa recalled Bill telling her, "I've had three years of college and I'm going to be a doctor." She recalled how convincing he was back in the early 1960's. "He could talk his way into or out of anything. He was very persuasive and, of course, I was very naive at the age of 19."

She was swept off her feet. Two months later, Teresa and Bill were married by a justice of the peace at Fort Sam Houston. On paper, the marriage lasted approximately three and a half years, until 1966, when Bill filed for a divorce that was granted in September. However, during those three and a half years, the young couple was separated numerous times by military commitments. The longest length of time they lived together as a married couple, according to Teresa, was a nine- to 10-month stretch in 1963 and 1964 when both were assigned to Fort Benning, Georgia.

Bill had been there a few months on a full-time basis and, since they were married, she received orders to Fort Benning when she completed training. They lived in a trailer park off base.

"Bill didn't show any signs to me that he was different or perverted while I was with him," Teresa said. "The only thing I remember now after all these things have come to pass was the late-night activity he had. Almost nightly he would want to go out for a run or take the dog for a walk. This would be at 10:30 or 11 every night. He'd come home some nights soaking wet with sweat as if he had been chased or something. If I asked why he was so sweaty, he'd just reply he'd had a good run or something. I was very trusting. Knowing what I know now, he was probably peeping in people's windows."

Teresa stated after being married a short time and living together at Fort Benning, Bill started to push her to get out of the Army. "He would tell me over and over again, 'No wife of mine is going to be in the service.' So after awhile I gave in and went along with his plan for me to go AWOL (absent without leave).

"His parents were living in the Portage Lakes area of Akron, Ohio. He sent me there to stay with them for 30 days. It was like I was some kind of criminal or something, being hidden away so the Army couldn't find me. After the 30 days, the Army gave me a discharge under general conditions, which at that time for a female wasn't a bad thing. However, when I look back on it, I really regret letting him talk me into that. I should never have gone along with that, but I was young and naïve. What can I say?"

I asked Teresa if Bill had ever been in trouble or disciplined while in the military. "Oh, yes. I'm sure he was.

Now I can't recall specifically, but there were times when he didn't go to work or we were going to separate schools and he'd tell me he was on suspension for one thing or another. He did, however, receive an honorable discharge in 1964."

After leaving the military, the couple moved to Michigan and stayed with Teresa's parents. Her father was skeptical of Bill, but had a good friend help Bill get a job at Ridgewood Hospital in Ypsilanti early in 1964.

"I'll never forget the night we were eating supper and my dad quizzed Bill about work at the hospital and what was going on there," Teresa said. "Bill answered him, and all of a sudden my dad called him a liar. My dad already knew Bill wasn't going to work and threw him out of the house, saying he didn't want his daughter around somebody like him. So Bill moved in with some guy he'd met at a bar and they shared a place nearby. Bill started calling me all the time to get back together.

"This was when the incident happened in Ypsilanti. When I agreed to get back with Bill, he wanted to get out of Michigan and move to Ohio. I was okay with it. He told me he had gotten in trouble and was arrested and put on probation. Before he could leave the state, I had to meet his probation officer and sign some paper saying I would be with him."

"Again, I was naïve. I believed his explanation that he was trying to steal some sheep from a guy's farm in Ypsilanti on a dare. So, when I met the probation officer, he asked if I knew what Bill had been arrested for, and I just blew it off and said, 'Yes, I know. He told me.' I signed the paper."

As a detective, I wanted to know more about the incident Teresa referred to in Ypsilanti, so I called the Michigan State Police and was able to get a copy of the incident reports that led to William Griffith's arrest and subsequent probation. Those events are as follows:

Burl Shriver of Belleville, Michigan, went to Ypsilanti Post 26 of the Michigan State Police on December 6, 1964, and told Trooper Dennis Payne that his neighbor, *Dave Rosenberg*, told him that Rosenberg's wife and daughter were looking out their window toward Shriver's house when they observed a white male looking in the window of Shriver's bathroom and his bedroom on December 2 at about 6:45 a.m. Shriver also said that Rosenberg's wife saw a white male walk to the road, wait a minute, and then get into an eastbound car that drove him away.

Shriver said that on December 4th his daughter, *Karen*, 17, saw shoe tracks in the snow that went around the house and appeared to be made by two persons. From the tracks, Shriver could tell that someone walked around the rear of the house, picked up a lawn chair, and brought it to the bathroom and bedroom windows.

No one was observed at Shriver's house on December 3rd. Shriver told the trooper that he felt the subject would return again since he had been there two out of the last three nights.

The vehicle described by Rosenberg's wife and daughter was a late-model white car with a dark convertible top. Shriver described the footprints in the snow as measuring 11¾-inches. Shriver told Trooper Payne that he would be watching for the prowler, and if he encountered him he was going to grab the individual and call the post for someone to come get him.

Payne said he would alert the other troopers on duty as to what was going on and that if they got a call to respond to Geddes Road they would know what to expect.

On December 7th at 6:30 a.m., Shriver called and asked the state police to respond to his residence because there were two guys walking around his yard. When troopers arrived, they found no one, but observed numerous tracks in the snow.

Shriver told one trooper that he thought one subject resembled a man who lived on the corner of Geddes and Barr roads.

The trooper spoke to the possible suspect, who claimed he had been in bed. The subject's father corroborated his son's story and nothing more was pursued.

On December 14th, at 6:35 a.m., Burl Shriver called Ypsilanti Post 26 to report he had captured a man peeping in his windows and that he was holding him until troopers arrived. Shriver told the dispatcher he recognized the man as being one of the men he had seen in his yard previously. He also added that on December 13th his daughter was shoveling snow and found in the driveway snow a pair of glasses in a carrying case.

Troopers arrived and took the subject to the post to interview him. Once on post, the man told troopers he had to be at work at 7:00 a.m. at Ridgewood Hospital where he was a lab technician.

The suspect was William E. Griffith Jr. He was 22, 6 feet 1 inches tall, weighed 165 pounds, and had blonde hair and blue eyes. Troopers released Griffith and told him to return to the post for further questioning when he completed his hospital shift.

Prior to the 3:30 p.m. interview, troopers spoke with Mrs. Rosenberg to see if she had seen anything that morning. Mrs. Rosenberg said that she saw a white car with a black convertible top slow down.

A subject was dropped off at Shriver's house and then the white car was driven down the road. The driver parked the car and then joined the man whom he had dropped off earlier.

Mrs. Rosenberg said that she and her children watched the first man look in a window of Shriver's house. All of a sudden Shriver ran outside and caught the one looking in his window. The other man got away. Mrs. Rosenberg said she could not see faces and could not identify anyone.

The eyeglass case that Shriver's daughter found had an address printed on it. Troopers took it to the Wayne Eye Clinic, at 35002 Michigan Avenue, in Wayne, Michigan. The receptionist checked the glasses out against the clinic's records. She determined they had been sold to William E. Griffith on October 20, 1964.

When Griffith returned to Post 26, he confessed to looking in the windows at the Shriver home and looking at Shriver's wife and daughter. A trooper noted in his report that Griffith was a married man, was quite agreeable, and in need of help. Griffith's vehicle was noted as a white 1964 Chevrolet convertible with a black top.

On December 15th, the trooper received authorization from Prosecuting Attorney Nicholas Wagner to charge Griffith with a complaint of disorderly person by window peeping. The next day, Justice of the Peace Ralph Foote issued the warrant and Griffith was charged. On December 23rd, Griffith pled guilty to the charge and was sentenced by Foote to 90 days in the Deheco Jail, with all the time suspended, one year of probation, and a $100.00 fine for the cost of probation.

After satisfying Bill's probation issues, Bill and Teresa Griffith moved to the Portage Lakes area near Akron, Ohio, in July 1965. Teresa was pregnant shortly after the move and then discovered Bill was seeing another woman named *Marilyn* (who later became the second Mrs. William E. Griffith). Teresa was devastated, and in October 1965 she left Bill and moved back to Michigan.

"I found out Bill got Marilyn pregnant while I was pregnant. They were working at the same hospital at the time in Akron. He chose Marilyn and asked me for a divorce. He did all the paperwork from Ohio and the divorce was granted in September 1966.

"I gave birth to our daughter, *Doris,* in March 1966. Bill never saw her or had any contact with her. The hardest thing for me was when Doris was 17 or 18 and started asking me who her real dad was. I just blew it off. Then you called me in late 1988 and said Bill was being sent to prison for rape and I thought I should tell Doris. I waited a few more years and told her who and where her father was. She would have been almost 27 when she learned who her real father was."

Teresa said Bill periodically stayed in touch with her into the 1970's. "He had a job with an insurance company and would come up to Westland and call to see if we could have lunch. My husband knew about it and it was okay. One time he (Bill) even wanted to see my mother so I called her and we had lunch at her house. Eventually Bill changed jobs and I never saw or heard from him again."

"Short of homicide, [rape] is the 'ultimate violation of self.'"

Byron R. White, former Associate Justice of the U.S. Supreme Court

Chapter 5

Marilyn Spencer was a stunning young lady. She, too, was swept off her feet by the fast-talking salesman and medical technician, William E. Griffith Jr. Marilyn said during an interview that she had given birth to their son, *Robert*, four months prior to marrying William Jr. She was not proud of that. She said that she was just naïve and young. Marilyn claimed she had no experience with men, let alone someone like Bill. She was head-over-heels in love with the young, dashing man and trusted him to make all their decisions.

"We rented an apartment in downtown Canton, and Bill stashed me away there. He controlled who I talked to and where I went. I look back on that time and it was like I was a prisoner," she recalled.

Marilyn told me the following story of a late-night phone call she received in May 1968 from Bill's father: "Bill's dad called to tell me Bill had been shot by a guy in Akron and that he was taken to St. Thomas Hospital, going into surgery, and it was touch and go. I asked him to come get me or for his wife to come and get me, but he said they didn't want to leave Bill's side. So here I was with a baby and having to get the neighbor lady to watch him so I could get a cab up to the hospital.

"I remember getting to the hospital and seeing detectives and policemen walking around and talking with one another, but no one would tell me anything. Bill's dad told me Bill had parked his car on some neighborhood street in Akron after having car trouble. He then started walking through yards to get to a main road and had cut through the yard of some 'gun nut,' who'd shot him three times."

Marilyn said she "could never understand why there were never any charges filed, or why she couldn't get a straight answer about what had happened. Later, in 1981 when Bill was in a counseling session for his voyeurism problem, he told me this guy shot him for peeping at his wife that night in May of 1968 and he (Bill) agreed not to sue the guy for shooting him if the guy wouldn't press charges. And that's how it was settled."

During my investigation into Griffith's activities during the summer of 1988, I contacted the records room at the Akron Police Department and obtained a copy of the shooting incident from 1968. The report revealed that between 12:21 a.m. and 1 a.m. May 3, 1968, the resident of 1289 Seward, *David Bosman,* shot William E. Griffith two times, after catching him peeping into windows and chasing him through yards.

Bosman told detectives he came home from working the afternoon shift at the Goodrich Company. His wife had gone out with girlfriends, so he had to walk the babysitter across the street to her house. He then went home to watch TV. Bosman said he went to the bathroom and heard something outside. He saw a male was by his garage looking through a window of his home. He called the babysitter and told her to call the police. He grabbed his .22-caliber revolver, which he had purchased four months earlier when he started working the afternoon shift. He told detectives that due to a rash of prowler activity in the neighborhood, he did not want to leave his wife unprotected when he was at work.

When he got outside, Bosman thought the prowler must have heard him because the man started to run away. Bosman said he yelled at the man to stop, but the man would not comply so he fired his gun in the air to scare him. That did not work so he fired four times at the man and thought he had struck him twice.

When detectives arrived at St. Thomas Hospital, they were able to interview Griffith. In his first story, Griffith claimed to have been drinking heavily that evening and he was in the area looking for a friend's house, but could not remember the friend's name. The detectives interviewing Griffith that early morning were familiar with him. Akron officers routinely filled out what were called "field interview cards" or "F. I. cards" when they came across a suspect or someone suspicious whom they didn't have enough evidence to formally charge with a crime. The cards were forwarded to the detective bureau. Those detectives interviewing Griffith were very familiar with the peeping tom and prowler calls that for months originated in the Seward Avenue neighborhood – the same neighborhood where William E. Griffith lived when he attended Perkins Junior High a decade earlier!

Detectives confronted Griffith with the fact that he had been identified on two prior field interview cards. On June 8, 1965, he was listed as a peeping tom suspect in the area of Carnegie and Sara Lee. On July 31, 1967, he was listed as a suspicious person in a prowler call in the area of 1128 Home Avenue.

Griffith then changed his story and told detectives he had been at a bar that evening, met a woman, and that he was looking for her. Detectives asked him why he ran away, if he was not doing anything wrong. Griffith said that Bosman had scared him. He thought he would have done the same thing if he were in Bosman's place. Then he said he did not wish to press charges. Griffith added that he had had an argument with his wife that night and they were not getting along and that was the reason he was not at home that night.

Griffith had been shot in the lower left portion of his back and in the upper right leg. He was in surgery for hours that morning and was listed in serious condition for a couple of days. Detectives confiscated Bosman's revolver and interviewed Bosman's wife. She told detectives that for weeks she had been plagued by prowlers around the house. Detectives conferred with Summit County prosecutors and charges never were filed. On the Akron Police Department report of this incident, William Griffith's place of employment was listed as Prudential Insurance.

Marilyn said her husband "always had a good job and was a good provider. The family never wanted for anything. Bill always had a job in sales or something that enabled him to travel or be out and about. He'd always had a love for cars and having his own car business."

Marilyn touched on the same strange nocturnal habits her husband exhibited as Teresa Martin had in earlier interviews. On an almost nightly basis, Bill would go out for a walk or run and not return for hours. They owned dogs all the time they were together. When he was an insurance man, he would say he had to meet a client who could only meet at that time due to hours the client worked. Later in their marriage, when Bill was refurbishing older or wrecked cars, he would tell Marilyn he had to go pick up a car he had put a bid on and the only hour he could get it was late at night.

Marilyn's comments mirrored Teresa's. "I was so naïve. For a couple of years in our marriage we got into cross-country skiing. Bill always had a lot of dark-colored ski masks around the house, so it wasn't out of the ordinary for him to have them. I can remember him coming home from business trips and giving the kids ski masks as gifts.

"The kids and I used to wash the family cars together in the summer months. I remember pulling ski masks and flashlights from underneath the car seats in the middle of summer. I never thought anything of it," Marilyn later wondered aloud. "We had fights over his late-night hours, but he always insisted it was work-related and I tried to be supportive of his job because he did so well at his sales jobs."

Marilyn told me that she knew of two times in their marriage when he had an affair. She had always insisted Bill get counseling, but he would not hear of it. She recalled two occasions in the early 1980's when Bill was arrested for voyeurism and the court ordered counseling. The counseling was provided through The Emerge Ministries on Mull Avenue in Akron.

She remembered the first counselor was a Dr. *Daniel Brooks,* who on one occasion had confronted her about Bill. Apparently, Dr. Brooks had some insight or had an indication from Bill during a counseling session that Griffith was doing more than mere window peeping. Griffith was perhaps raping women as well. Marilyn said that at the time she was furious with Dr. Brooks, and the doctor never broached the subject again. Marilyn said that she would not entertain any nonsense like that at the time. However, based on Griffith's future actions, Dr. Brooks proved to be prophetic.

After early counseling sessions, Dr. Brooks resigned from The Emerge Ministries and took a job with the Missouri prison system as a criminal psychologist. Bill's counseling sessions were turned over to Dr. *Dean Edwards,* who agreed, as a favor to Dr. Brooks, to take Bill as a patient. Edwards told me in the summer of 1988 that Brooks had confided to him that "Bill is a special case."

Marilyn said there were times in their marriage, while the children were growing up, when Bill had mood swings related to his parents. Marilyn said Bill would drink and argue with his father. He then took out his frustrations on their oldest son, Robert, by striking him and verbally berating him. When he argued with his mother or was not getting along with her, Bill would take it out on her (Marilyn).

"Bill's family never really accepted me," Marilyn said, "and tried on numerous occasions to break us up. Bill and his father would always reference 'knowing people' or having friends in organized crime who would do favors for them if they needed it. They always intimidated me through fear. I had no way of knowing what was true or not. Some of the characters Bill associated with when he was running his car business were very seedy. I insisted to him that I didn't want them around the house or the children."

Marilyn pointed out that Bill's father was very knowledgeable when it came to electronics. "His father worked as a television repairman when I first met him. Bill's uncle owned a TV repair shop in Akron. Bill's father showed Bill how to repair and install telephones, too. I remember watching him take a phone apart and put it back together once, using just a butter knife instead of a screwdriver."

Bill's knowledge of telephones would prove interesting in the future investigation of dozens of home break-ins and rapes.

AS DEFINED BY THE OHIO REVISED CODE
2907.02

Rape-(A) (1) No person shall engage in sexual conduct with another who is not the spouse of the offender... (A) (2) No person shall engage in sexual conduct with another when the offender purposely compels the other person to submit by force or threat of force. Violation is a felony of the first degree, punishable by a minimum of 10 years' incarceration and a maximum of 25 years' incarceration.

CHAPTER 6

When one looks at William E. Griffith Jr.'s life, decade by decade, I think the 1970's would have to be considered the proverbial calm before the storm that rocked the 1980's. Earlier Griffith had sexually experimented with a couple of boys in his youth, and developed an addiction to masturbation and voyeurism at age 16. Bill's wives informed me of his constant nocturnal activity. Then there was the arrest by Michigan State Police in Ypsilanti, his appearance on field interview cards by Akron police in 1965 and 1967, and his shooting by an alert Akron homeowner in 1968. The 1970's also revealed that Bill's name would pop up on the radar screen of authorities in Stark County.

In the late 1960's, Bill moved his young family from Akron and Summit County to the northern part of Stark County – Canton and Uniontown. Bill had good jobs in the insurance industry and supported his family well. He also began to bid for vehicles at auctions and purchased a wrecker to tow these cars back to a garage, which he and some business associates operated so they could refurbish the cars for sale.

A review of file cards from the Stark County Sheriff's Office indicated Bill was a suspect in some criminal incidents during the 1970's. During the winter of 1974, Bill was listed as a suspect in the theft of an auxiliary sheriff's badge from inside a 1969 Ford van. The vehicle had been parked at the Moose Club in Canton. There was no other information available. Also in 1974, William E. Griffith Jr. was listed as a suspect in the forgery of a check at Harter Bank in Canton.

In 1975, there was a more in-depth incident report taken by Stark County Sheriff's Sgt. Charlie Branch. It appeared there were numerous reports of "peeping tom" incidents around the Uniontown-Hartville area. The complaints led one neighborhood group to conduct their own patrol to watch for a man peeping into the windows of homes. On the summer evening of July 18th, several residents gathered at the Market Avenue North home of *Steven Foster*, whose daughter had seen someone looking in her bedroom window just before midnight.

Several men, along with Foster, walked around the houses searching for the nighttime prowler. They had no luck in locating him. However, they located a suspicious vehicle. No one knew who owned the late model Thunderbird parked near the Foster residence. The group called the sheriff's office and asked for a deputy to be dispatched. Sgt. Branch responded, took a report from Foster, and was shown the vehicle. Branch, along with the residents, decided to watch the vehicle to see if anyone entered the car. After two and half hours of waiting (you won't find that kind of service anymore), a male figure emerged from the darkness between two houses and got into the car. Branch approached the car and told the driver to stop.

Branch identified the subject as William E. Griffith Jr. of 1067 Peony Street in Hartville. Griffith told Branch that he had driven through the area earlier and his car had overheated, so he parked it to let it cool down while he walked home. Once home, he watched some TV and then went to retrieve his car and return home. Branch shined his flashlight in the car and questioned Griffith about several wigs in the front seat. Griffith said the wigs belonged to his wife. Without enough evidence to file charges, Branch filed his report without further action being taken.

During the mid- to late-1970's, as rapes were occurring in Stark County and in neighboring communities, I was attending Canton Central Catholic High School. Besides a lot of socializing, I played football and ran track. There was always somewhere to go and something to do with friends, whether at the mall, school or someone's house.

It was also a time when co-ed classmates earned extra money by babysitting, even though, in light of all the news reports of rapes, they were concerned for their own safety. Subsequently, they would ask me and other friends to call or stop by while they were babysitting because the rapist might be lurking nearby. I called plenty of girls as they were watching someone's children. Or I would stop at houses where the girls were babysitting. Sometimes stopping by had to be done covertly because the sitter did not have permission for anyone to be there. However, the contact was a risk worth taking to make sure everyone was safe.

Some of the girls came right out and said they were scared when watching small kids because the young went to bed early and then the sitters were by themselves until the parents returned. For other girls, this part of babysitting was just plain socializing on the phone, which was a big part of high school life then. During my senior year, I remember girls exchanging stories about being spooked with the peeping tom incidents which some of them experienced when babysitting. I no longer recall where those homes were. I do know that, after these stories started circulating, some of my friends and I toyed with the idea of scaring some girls. Looking back now, I'm glad we decided not to be pranksters.

I recall that there was legitimate and palpable fear among these girls when they thought someone had been outside in the bushes watching them while babysitting. Some would call a parent to come sit with them, or some would call the local police. No one incident stands out. I also remember mothers spoke with their daughters at school functions about being careful and staying together as a group because of a concern that some pervert could be watching females.

My mother would come home from the hospital (where she worked as a registered nurse) and speak about women she worked with whose daughters babysat and how scared these girls were.

While growing up, voyeurism and rape were just stories to me. After graduating from high school, I enlisted in the U.S. Air Force for four years and subsequently was honorably discharged as a security policeman. I joined the Perry Township Police Department in Stark County and then moved to the Jackson Township force a year later (in 1983) when offered a full-time position.

During my orientation at Jackson on the midnight shift, I trained with the supervisor, Sgt. Claude Keeton. He took me to the area bounded by Portage Street on the north, Lorraine Street on the east, Dale Avenue on the west and Rob Street on the south. This rectangular area was the scene of several burglaries and rapes in the early 1980's.

Sgt. Keeton told me stories about the rapist's method repeated time and again. He said police never came up with a good suspect and did not know if the rapist lived in that relatively small area. He felt the only way the case ever would be solved would be when the rapist miscalculated and picked a house with a gun-toting lady, who would blow the guy away when he came into the bedroom.

Sgt. Keeton added that rapes occurred in other locations in Stark County as well, with the same method of operation. He told me that if I was assigned this area for patrol on midnights I should park at a nearby church when I took my lunch or took any kind of break and watch for someone wandering around on foot. He felt this could give detectives the break they needed to identify the rapist. This was the first time I heard the phrase "the Rob Street Rapist." That phrase was used to describe the man who had been raping women in this allotment since 1980.

Once released from orientation, I started working the midnight shift. I remembered Keeton's admonition to park in that church lot when I took breaks. I never saw anyone or anything move. While sitting there I did have a flood of memories about the girls I knew during high school who were afraid of a peeping tom in the bushes and who wanted their friends to call or stop by. I wondered what connection all this had to the man caught years later.

From my interviews with Teresa Martin, Bill's first wife, I learned Bill worked for the Prudential Insurance Company during this time period. Bill made numerous business trips back to Michigan. I learned from Teresa that Bill had called her on more than one occasion to get together for dinner or lunch. Bill never asked to meet his daughter, Doris. A few years after divorcing Teresa, Bill allowed her new husband to adopt Doris. Bill never had contact with Doris as she was raised by her mother and stepfather.

As a detective conducting my background investigation into William Griffith, I checked with agencies about places where I knew Bill had traveled. One of those areas was Westland, Michigan, where Teresa worked and lived and raised Doris. I spoke with Detective Laura Moore of the Westland Police Department, and told her about my investigation of Griffith and his modus operandi. I asked the detective if there were any unsolved cases from back in the '70s or '80s that would fit with Griffith. I also told her I knew Griffith was in her city.

Detective Moore told me about a place in Westland called Hampton Court Apartments. This complex of apartments and townhomes was the scene of a series of indecent exposures, obscene phone calls and attempted sexual assaults. Moore strongly believed all these incidents were the work of one perpetrator. She was never able to solve the crimes, but they reflected a similar method of operation used by William Griffith. Subsequently, I was sent a series of reports by the Westland PD with details of some of those incidents. None of the incidents cultivated any physical evidence that could be used to positively link Griffith to those crimes.

I have included the information about Westland's unsolved sex crimes because of information from a source I developed during the course of the investigation. The source had been with Bill at the Golden Valley Health Center in Golden Valley, Minnesota, while Griffith was eluding authorities. The source indicated that Griffith would go back to Michigan to watch his daughter as she grew up. He knew he could not contact her; however, he had to see her. One thing I learned through the course of this investigation was that wherever William E. Griffith Jr. spent any length of time, incidents of voyeurism and/or rape increased after his arrival.

THE
ATTACKS
1980-1988

"Many rapists feel compelled to commit these crimes and are not able to stop themselves...other than date rape, I would assume that 90 percent of rapes are committed by serial rapists..."

Ronald M. Holmes, Professor of Criminology at University of Louisville in Kentucky
Akron Beacon Journal, September 11, 1988

Chapter 7

As a new decade began, Detective Laura Moore was trying to develop a suspect for a rash of sex crimes in Westland, Michigan. Police agencies in Stark County, Ohio, began to investigate incidents of rape that involved single women who lived alone or with a young child. The rapes occurred during the early morning hours by a ski-masked intruder who carried a flashlight and a knife. The ski-masked rapist cut telephone lines outside the residences and created an escape route for himself prior to attacking his victims.

In 1980, there were eight attacks which fit the above method of operation. They occurred in separate jurisdictions in Stark County and each police agency worked its cases with very little sharing of information. No one recognized the pattern at this early stage. However, there were two attacks in 1980 where the police recovered latent fingerprints that would be valuable later in unmasking the rapist.

July 23, 1980

On a hot July night, Bill told Marilyn he had to go pick up a car he had bought at auction and planned to restore. Marilyn was used to Bill's comings and goings at late hours and thought nothing of it. Bill was primed for his activity this night. He had his eye on a vulnerable young female. His plan was perfect. She lived alone and there was no male who visited her. Bill had done his homework for months, watching

Debbie Waltz come home from work and go out on the weekends. Perhaps he even thought that she would be easier than the last two victims.

Debbie Waltz lived in a duplex on Edelweiss Street Northeast in Plain Township, near North Canton. The neighborhood in Diamond Estates consisted of duplexes for several blocks. Debbie, 22, felt a sense of independence living on her own for the first time. On July 23rd, Debbie went to bed after watching the evening news. She was awakened by a hand pressed over her mouth and a bright light shining in her eyes. She caught a glimpse of her alarm clock: it was 4 a.m.

Bill wore a dark-colored ski mask as he put a knife against her throat and told her not to scream. He told her that if she cooperated she would not be hurt, and added that a friend named Dick was in the next room with a gun.

Bill ordered her to take off her clothing. As she complied, he kept the flashlight trained on her. Once she was naked, he told her to lie down on the bedroom floor. Debbie lay there as Bill lowered his pants and stared at her. Debbie closed her eyes and wished for everything to be over. She thought this had to be a dream. Within moments she felt him slide inside her. She was repulsed and horrified. Several times during the assault, Bill ordered her not to look at him.

Debbie told Stark County sheriff's deputies later that it felt as if the rapist put something like saran wrap over her vagina before he raped her. She said it felt funny when he thrust back and forth and it made a sound like some type of plastic covering. Her attacker raped her for what Debbie estimated was a half hour. When the rapist was finished, Bill warned her not to call the police and that he and Dick would be watching her. Debbie told deputies that at no time did Dick answer her attacker. She had no idea if anyone else was present.

Bill thought it was a stroke of genius to act as if he had someone else with him. It would keep the police guessing. He was very proud of himself, felt superior to everyone else and believed he would not be caught because he put so much planning into it. He had graduated from peeping and mere masturbation. He was fulfilling *all* of his fantasies.

As they processed the crime scene, deputies discovered that a living room front window had been pried open and a 16-gallon keg had been used as a step stool to boost the rapist to gain entry. The keg had been dragged to the window from a neighbor's car port. Deputies drove Debbie to the hospital where medical personnel obtained a rape kit. Deputies requested that Stark County Crime Lab technicians respond to the scene. It later proved to be a wise decision, as lab personnel lifted a latent fingerprint from the window where entry was made. It was Bill's first major mistake. He had raped only a few women at this point and planned out every detail thoroughly – watching, waiting and rehearsing again and again. He had no idea he had touched the glass with his gloveless hand. He would relive his attack along with others for nights afterward, fantasizing, reliving and reveling in his domination and how frightened his victims had been. He never felt stronger, more emboldened or more fulfilled than he did now.

The latent print was placed into evidence at the crime lab where it stayed for over eight years until a comparison to a known suspect was requested. In 1980, the only way to identify an unknown latent print was to compare it to the fingerprint card of a known offender. There was no computerized fingerprint file in use at this time in the United States. It was not until 1997 when Stark County began using AFIS (Automated Fingerprint Identification System).

November 16, 1980

Bill stepped up his activity in the fall, whether due to the crisp autumn air or his success with more than a half dozen rapes. Twice he attacked in October and twice in November.

Bill loved the Frances Acres allotment in Jackson Township. The rectangular geographical formation was lined with approximately 20 brick duplexes, all uniform in appearance, construction and with the same floor plan. If he knew how to get into one, he knew how to get into *all* of them!

On this November evening, Bill had told Marilyn that he had to meet a client for his insurance job and because of the client's schedule they had to meet at night. Again, Marilyn was wary of the late-night hours three or more nights a week, but she remained silent.

Bill set out for Jackson Township from his home in Hartville. Shortly after midnight he arrived at the planned parking spot in the same allotment as his intended victim. He tried to blend right in with all the other parked cars.

Once parked, Bill made his way to *Mary Westover's* duplex and saw that she had her car parked in the connected carport. Mary Westover was 23, single, and lived in her own place just a couple of miles from her parents' home. She had been out the night before her assault. She got into bed after 1 a.m. Bill took a couple of hours to check out more potential victims as he watched and waited.

At 3:45 a.m., Bill was ready. He cut the telephone line outside the duplex, gently forced and removed the glass pane on the front storm door, and made entry to Mary's residence. He left the door ajar for a quick escape and took the receiver from the phone on the kitchen wall and stuffed it inside the gutter at the rear side of the duplex. Bill came back inside and made his way to Mary's bedroom. Mary was awakened by a masked man shining a light in her eyes. He told her he had a gun. "We won't hurt you," he said, but Mary never saw anyone else.

Bill asked Mary her age and ordered her into the living room. He ordered her to disrobe while he shined a light up and down her body before raping her vaginally. Bill lived for this particular moment when he made his victim strip in front of him. He was in total control. During her attack, Mary remembered that her attacker asked if she was hurt or uncomfortable. Mary, like the others before her, was ordered to stay still in her bedroom for 20 minutes and not to call the police. Mary watched her alarm clock intently waiting for the time to pass. Her attacker left at 4:17 a.m.

When Jackson Township police arrived, they took Mary to a local hospital emergency room. Her rape kit was provided later.

Jackson police were using the services of the Ohio Bureau of Criminal Investigation (BCI) to process crime scenes. BCI dispatched a technician who discovered that the phone lines had been cut outside the residence and the telephone receiver from the kitchen had been stuffed in the gutter. The technician was able to lift two latent fingerprints from a pane of glass on the front storm door where the attacker made his entrance and exit. For the second time in 1980, Bill had made a major mistake.

By year's end, Bill had promised himself that 1981 was going to be even better. He had an array of targets to choose from with so many allotments of duplexes, apartments and trailer parks which provided affordable housing for young women who were striking out on their own. Bill was spending two to three nights a week out and about, watching and waiting; waiting and watching in order to find the right victim to satisfy his lust. Other than the two attacks that took place in the Diamond Estates allotment, no one knew the eight rapes were the work of one man, one single ski-masked rapist.

January 23, 1981

Authorities believe Bill started his 1981 sexual assaults early. He returned to one of his favorite areas, Frances Acres in Jackson Township. *Donna Bertram* lived on Portage Street in one of the brick duplexes that littered the allotment. She loved the large yards that each duplex had. She was 21 and on her own for the first time in her young life.

Bill had been keeping an eye on her since he had attacked Mary Westover two and a half months before. He left his Hartville residence after giving Marilyn another late-night excuse. He parked his car in the same inconspicuous manner as before. Bill was very proud of the planning for his attacks. He had not drawn attention to himself.

He stood in the bushes for an hour on the cold early morning of January 23rd before he entered her home. At 5:25 a.m., Donna awakened to find Bill standing over her. He clasped his hand over her mouth, shined a light in her eyes and ordered her not to scream. Bill pressed the knife to her throat and told her that he and his friends had knives and guns and that they would use them if she did not do as she was told.

Bill ordered her out of bed and into the living room. He ordered her to take off her clothes and to lie on the floor, where he raped her vaginally. Like the others before her, Donna was told to lie in her room and stay there for 20 minutes. Donna did as she was told. When she tried to call the police, she discovered that the phones were dead.

Donna dressed and ran to her neighbors' and told them what happened. The Jackson Township police were called. Upon arrival, the police took Donna to the hospital where a rape kit was provided for evidentiary purposes.

The BCI technician who responded to the scene lifted two latent fingerprints from the glass on the rear kitchen door and one from a window over the kitchen sink. Underneath the kitchen window was a cement block authorities surmised was used to boost himself through the window.

As in similar attacks, the phone lines were cut and a receiver was taken from the kitchen and put in the gutter on the roof. However, this time the BCI technician discovered a shoe impression by a bedroom window. The print had a pleated design. No one knew if this was from the attacker's shoe. The technician made a plaster cast of the print for evidence.

Much like other rape victims' statements to Jackson Township police, Donna described her attacker as having a deep voice and wearing an orange and black ski jacket with dark pants and a dark ski mask.

April 18, 1981

Bill's insurance job provided him with not only a car for his use, but also a lot of time on the road. He took advantage of the time and drove aimlessly for hours from one county to another. He located his victims during these times. When a female caught his eye, she became a potential victim. He spent countless hours on his own special kind of surveillance by window peeping. Bill would drive by a potential target at various times of the day and during different days of the week to make sure when his target would be alone.

Bill was methodical and did his homework. On days or evenings when he was unable to drive by to check on a potential victim, he would make an obscene phone call or simply call and hang up. He always checked to see when victims were alone. On occasion he would make obscene calls just for fun.

In the early spring, Bill knew it was time to take the young lady he had been watching in Portage County's Suffield Township. She had caught his eye one day when he saw her in her driveway by the Suffield IGA grocery store on

State Route 43. The store's parking lot provided him with convenient parking for the task at hand on April 18th.

Jill Davis lived in a duplex next to the Suffield IGA. Jill's home was plain, with an attached single-car garage and a beautiful apple tree in the front yard. The apple tree was a big reason Jill wanted to move there.

She was 23 when Bill Griffith wore a ski mask, placed his gloved hand over her mouth and held a knife against her throat early on April 18th. He told her not to scream or he would kill her. Jill complied with his demands.

Bill told her to take off her nightgown while he shined a light over her naked body and told her to lie on the floor. Bill raped her vaginally. Afterwards, he told her to lie in her bed and not move while he took some of her things. Jill lay motionless for what seemed like hours when she finally decided to call the Portage County Sheriff's Office, but her phone was not working. She dressed and ran to a neighbor, begging them to call the sheriff because she had been raped.

When deputies arrived and surveyed the crime scene, they found that the outside phone lines had been cut. They also found that a pry bar was used to force entry to the front window. A screen from Jill's bedroom window was found twisted and thrown onto the roof.

Jill said her attacker was in his late 20s, 6 feet tall and about 190 pounds. No other evidence was located.

From the beginning of 1981until the end of April there were also three other rapes of single women living alone that fit the pattern Bill had set for himself. In another similar attack, the victim refused to remove her clothes and screamed. Griffith fled.

August 31, 1981

The following two attacks attributed to William

Edward Griffith Jr. marked the first known time he struck twice in the same evening.

Carolyn Cook was 30 and lived in the same apartment that had been occupied by *Jane Luckring* when she was victimized nine months earlier on Baier Circle Northeast in North Canton. It was 3:45 a.m. when a strange noise woke Cook. She started down the stairs to investigate the sound and saw a shadowy figure at her back kitchen door. The subject was using some type of tool to try to open the door. Carolyn went back to her bedroom, opened the window and looked down at the man at her back door. He heard the window open and looked up at Carolyn. The would-be attacker ran off.

Carolyn later notified the Stark County Sheriff's Office. She said the prowler was a white male with a stocky build who wore a stocking cap. She said this was the second time someone had tried to break in since she had moved in.

Marianne Jenkins was 26, divorced, and living with her infant daughter and toddler son on Zircon Street Northeast in Diamond Estates, the same neighborhood of prior attacks. It was 5:20 a.m. when a man wearing a dark ski mask placed a gloved hand over her mouth and shined a light in her eyes to wake her. The attacker told Marianne he had a gun, though he never showed her one. If she did not do as ordered, he said he would kill her baby in the next room.

The attacker pulled back the covers and saw she was sleeping in the nude. He shined his flashlight up and down her body and told her to close her eyes and not look at him. He called out to an unknown person in the next room, but Marianne never heard anyone answer.

The intruder rubbed Marianne's vagina and penetrated her with his fingers. After a few moments, the attacker told her to lie still for 20 minutes and not to call the police. The male attacker then called out to an unknown person, "Come on, let's get out of here."

Marianne heard a car start on Zircon Street. She leaped from her bed and ran into the other bedroom where both children were asleep. She tried to call the sheriff's office; however, the phone line was dead.

Stark County Crime Lab technicians processed the scene. Crime Lab personnel were able to lift a latent fingerprint from the disabled telephone in the kitchen. The attacker had left the receiver on the kitchen table. Nothing else of evidentiary value was developed.

Marianne told her interviewer that she had received an obscene phone call the day before the attack. The caller asked her what color panties she was wearing. She hung up. The caller phoned back twice more, each time asking the same question. She said the caller's voice was the same as that of her attacker. All involved believed the attacker had been watching Marianne for some time before the break-in.

She described her attacker as a white male, 6 feet tall with a husky build, who weighed 200 pounds. He wore blue jeans and a dark-colored long-sleeve shirt. The ski mask had yellow around the eye slits.

In December 1981, and again on January 23, 1982, Marianne called the sheriff's office to report phone calls she had received. The male voice was identical to the voice in the calls she had received prior to being raped. On each of these occasions the caller asked her the same question, "Do you still sleep in the nude? I'll come back and lick your pussy again. I know you liked it."

For the remainder of 1981, there were no more reported attacks in the northeast Ohio area. That may have been because William Griffith was involved with the justice system in Ravenna, Ohio, because of a voyeurism incident, or because he may have found another area in which to prowl.

<u>February 10, 1982</u>

Savanah Taylor was 28 and lived on 37th Street Northeast in Canton. She and her husband had lived there for a couple of years and never had any problems with neighbors or anyone else. Her husband worked midnights at J&L Steel in nearby Louisville. She had received several obscene phone calls around Thanksgiving 1981, but never reported them to the police.

Sometime between 4 a.m. and 5 a.m., Savanah was awakened when her face was shoved down in her pillow and held there. The male voice told her not to scream, to do what she was told and she would not get hurt. The man then let her up and told her he was just going to take a few things. He ordered her to lead him downstairs to the living room.

Once downstairs, the masked man ordered her to take off her clothes. Savanah complied while the man shined a flashlight on her. The man told her he was going to rape her and for her to lie on the floor. Her attacker lowered his pants and stood over her and ordered her to "suck me." Savanah said, "No, I don't know how." The attacker put a knife against her throat, and forced her to comply with his demand. The sheer horror of being awakened from a deep sleep and forced to take a man in her mouth caused Savanah to tremble with fear and revulsion. As Savanah complied with her attacker, he remarked, "You are easy – not like the others."

The attacker ejaculated in her mouth and performed cunnilingus. He ordered Savanah to go up to her room and be still for 20 minutes while "we take a few things." Savanah heard her attacker leave and tried to call the police, but the phone line was dead. When deputies arrived, they saw where the phone lines were cut and found pry marks on the aluminum storm door where entry had been made.

Savanah described her attacker as a white male, 5 feet 11, who wore a green, long-sleeve plaid flannel shirt, a gray coat with gold lining, blue jeans and a dark-blue ski mask with yellow striping around the eye and nose holes. She said he spoke in a low voice, yet very firm. She said she saw the suspect's legs, which were extremely white as if the subject never got any sunlight. She noted a strange odor from his body, not like normal body odor. He smelled as if he had just had sex. Deputies found her kitchen phone receiver on the roof. A few days later, Savanah called deputies to say that three steak knives were missing.

Our investigation revealed that during 1982 Griffith was involved in an additional four rapes in North Canton, Uniontown, Jackson Township and Canton. The attacks followed the same pattern as those in 1980 and 1981.

May 12, 1983

It is not known if Bill's job training or family matters explain why he did not attack women for certain lengths of time. I always believed that Griffith threw himself into the hunting and cultivation of more victims whenever he had the time.

Pamela Alley lived in the infamous Diamond Estates neighborhood on Edelweiss Street in Plain Township. At 3:30 a.m., a white male, about 5 feet 10 to 6 feet tall, slim build, possibly in his late 20s to 30s, who wore a dark sweater, ski mask and surgical gloves, woke her by placing a hand over her mouth and shining a light in her eyes. The attacker had a knife against her throat when he told her in a soft, firm voice, "Don't scream or I'll kill you and your kid."

The attacker had her lead him downstairs to the living room where he ordered her to take off her clothes and get on the floor. Pam was raped and ordered to go back upstairs and lie still. The attacker told her that he and Keith were going to take a few things. Pam did not see or hear anyone else. Responding deputies discovered that the phone lines were cut and the phone receiver from the kitchen was hidden under the cushion of a chair in the living room. The crime lab developed three latent fingerprints at the scene.

August 31, 1983

Diane Mullroy lived on Portage Street Northwest in Bill's favorite Jackson Township neighborhood, Frances Acres, when a ski- masked man woke her out of a sound sleep. The attacker showed her he had a gun from the light of his flashlight. The attacker raped her vaginally on the floor.

Diane described her attacker as a white male, 6 feet tall in his early 30s, who wore dark clothing and a dark ski mask. Diane also detected an odor coming from the attacker but could not place it.

April 28, 1984

Almost eight months passed before Griffith's next attack. *Monica Rand*, 25, lived on Turquoise Street Northeast in Plain Township's Diamond Estates. Monica was the fifth victim Griffith abused at Diamond Estates. At 2:30 a.m., she was awakened by a man wearing a dark ski mask and touched her arm, startling her. He showed her a long-barreled blue-steel revolver with light-colored grips. Her attacker pulled down her covers and shined his light up and down her naked body.

"Bitch, get up and go downstairs" he told her. The attacker then told her to get on her knees in the living room and ordered her to perform oral sex. Monica complied and then was told to lie back while her attacker performed oral sex on her before raping her vaginally. Monica was ordered upstairs and told to stay still for one hour and not to call the police.

Monica told deputies her attacker had a difficult time maintaining an erection during the ordeal. She described her attacker as a white male, age 30 to 35, about 6 feet tall and 200 pounds with a husky build, who wore a black ski mask and other dark clothing. He spoke with a low, firm voice.

"It's time for honest language. When a man has sex with a frightened, beaten and intimidated woman there is only one word to describe it, and that is RAPE."

-- Denis MacShane, British politician

Chapter 8

From 1985 through 1988 we witnessed the same mode of operation again and again. And not just in Stark County, but also in Summit County and even Miami County south of Dayton. Bill was no doubt full of himself at this point – but unbeknownst to him – he had left his fingerprints at several scenes up to this date and his very own prints were on file with police departments in two counties. By the start of the summer of 1985, Bill had decided to explore a new venue for victims, being very familiar with Summit County and the Akron/Fairlawn area where he grew up.

In June 1985, a Fairlawn resident, 25, on Chamberlain Road was the first of four victims whose cases fit the mode of operation of Bill Griffith. She told police that her attacker wore a mask, gloves and dark clothing and threatened her with a knife. He also threatened to return and kill the victim if she called the police.

It was obvious to investigators that there always was a plan when the attacker set out to conquer his prey. If the plan could not be acted on due to unforeseen circumstances, he had a backup plan. Bill spent many hours stalking his victims so he could go from one to the other in a seamless transition in a small geographic area if need be.

In all of the Fairlawn incidents, screens were removed from windows and mangled. Most were tossed onto the roofs of the apartments as in Stark County, just a few miles to the south. Another similarity was the disabling of the telephones. It appeared the two counties were looking for the same individual. Bill was very familiar with Fairlawn, which was just west of Akron where he grew up and attended high school. Bill traveled the area extensively for his employment, including neighboring Portage County. Bill was very confident that local law enforcement agencies were not sharing information on rape cases, let alone initiating discussions about one particular suspect.

It was during a 1988 interview that I had with Bill Griffith's father that I discovered it was at about this time that Bill started a job for a company in Oklahoma City, Oklahoma. He was hired as a salesman and manager for a pollution clean-up company called USPCI. The company sold cleaning equipment to industrial and manufacturing companies around the United States.

Bill was doing very well in his new job and traveled constantly during the week to service accounts. He would come home on weekends. He had an apartment in Sayre, Oklahoma, just to have a place to sleep when he was not calling on clients. Bill had a Diner's Club credit card, courtesy of USPCI, for travel expenses, airline tickets, rental cars, motel stays or meals. Bill preferred to drive in order to widen the scope of his attacks, and it opened up a whole new area in southwest Ohio.

April 30, 1986

Stacey Marks was 22 and lived on Wisteria Lane in Troy, Ohio, in Miami County. The large apartment complex, spread over a few hundred acres, was highly visible to any motorist traveling the nearby interstate highway. Stacey liked the apartment location because her mother lived only two doors from her. Since she had two small children, it was nice having her mother close.

Stacey's husband was in the U.S. military and stationed in Okinawa, Japan. Stacey had put the children to bed for the evening and watched some TV before falling asleep on the couch.

Sometime after 2:30 a.m., Bill placed a hand over her mouth and a knife against her throat and told her, "Scream and I'll kill you." Bill told her he would not hurt her daughter asleep on the floor in front of the TV. He slowly started to move his hand away from her mouth when she gasped, and he quickly put it back, and warned her through gritted teeth, "I'll kill your daughter."

Bill then had Stacey walk into her bedroom. He ordered her to take off her clothes and get on the floor. Stacey complied and Bill said, "I'm not going to rape you. I want you to give me head." Stacey told him, "I can't do that." "Why not?" Bill demanded. "I have herpes," she said. "Honest to God? You're kidding?" Bill said incredulously. "No," she said. "I wouldn't kid about something like that."

Bill told her to get her daughter and bring her back into the bedroom and to stay there for an hour while he took her television set and other things. Stacey complied, waited for more than an hour, and then mustered up enough courage to see if her attacker was gone.

When she found he had fled, she went to her mother's and asked her to call the police. Stacey told Miami County deputies that her attacker was tall, about 6 feet, and was dressed all in dark clothes, including a ski mask. Entry was made to her apartment by prying the laundry room door. Her phone receiver was taken and never found. Stacey added that the attacker carried a flashlight.

June 28, 1986

Shirley Green lived on Honeysuckle Drive in Troy, Ohio, in the same area as Stacey Marks. At 1:30 a.m., Shirley, 27, was awakened on her couch by a man, who wore a ski mask and had his hand over her mouth with a light shining in her eyes. "Don't scream or I'll shoot you and your children," Bill dead-panned.

"He told me to get up and to go into the front room. When we got there, he told me to take my clothes off and lie down." Shirley later told police her attacker told her to masturbate while he shined the flashlight on her. After a few moments, he made her lift her legs in the air, and he performed oral sex on her before he inserted his penis inside her and ejaculated. When he finished, he told her to get dressed, go to her room and stay there while he took some things.

Shirley waited a few moments and went back in the front room and called out, "Are you there?" No one answered. She shut the front door that had been left open. In the living room, she tried to call the sheriff, but the phone had been disabled. She went back to her bedroom and was able to call the sheriff from there. A rape kit was completed and the scene was processed.

Shirley described her attacker as a white male, 5 feet 8 and about 180 pounds. She never saw a gun. The deputies found that the attacker came in through an unlocked garage door. Shirley was married and her husband worked midnights. The deputies believed her attacker had been watching her for a few weeks.

July 10, 1986

Melanie Piper lived on Honeysuckle Drive in Troy and was 23. At 4:10 a.m., she was awakened when Bill Griffith tapped her on the head with a flashlight and said, "Don't make a sound and I won't hurt you. Otherwise, I'll have to hurt you."

She said that she was incoherent and did not know what was going on, so he prodded her to get up and go into the family room. He ripped the cord off of the phone in that room. She started to whimper when her attacker told her to shut up and show him where her other phones were.

She showed him a phone in the kitchen, but not the one in her bedroom. He took the receiver from the kitchen phone. She saw that the living room window had been opened and figured that was how he got in. Bill took her to her spare bedroom and told her to take off her clothes. Melanie argued with him before he told her he would hurt her, so she took off her nightgown and he shined the light on her. He told her to lie down and give him head.

Melanie began to cry. Bill yelled at her to shut up, and performed oral sex on her before raping her vaginally. Once finished, he told her to get her clothes on, go to her room and not leave for 20 minutes while he and a friend took some things. This was a line he had not used for a few years – a reference to another person – a ploy that he originated while operating in his home county of Stark.

Melanie never saw anyone else. "I've been watching you for awhile," Bill told her. Melanie told deputies that when she had mowed her lawn a couple nights before she had noticed footprints in the mulch around her bedroom window. Melanie told deputies that her attacker was 5 feet 9 and had a firm, athletic build like a runner. He wore dark clothing, including a dark-colored ski mask. He was a white male with blue eyes.

In 1986, Miami County sheriff's deputies reported that for a six-month period their calls regarding prowlers and obscene phone calls had been extremely high. They knew someone was stalking the area that included Wysteria Lane and Honeysuckle Drive where some 250 homes were located. Mid-July 1986, Miami County investigators read a teletype sent over the National Crime Information Computer (NCIC) by the Fairlawn Police Department in Summit County, Ohio.

Fairlawn Detective Michael Smith was investigating a

series of rapes and break-ins in his community and listed the *modus operandi (m.o.)*. Miami County officials recognized the similarities and called Smith. He advised them that the Fairlawn attacks occurred in 1985 and that he was in contact with authorities from Stark County, including Canton, Alliance and North Canton police, Jackson Township police and the Stark County Sheriff's Office. All of these agencies had experienced break-ins when women were raped by a man wearing a ski mask. The detectives involved agreed to continue to exchange information and ideas on how to solve the attacks.

August 20, 1986

At 24, *Erin Olson* lived on Monterey Boulevard in North Canton. Erin was startled when awakened at 5 a.m. by a man with a gloved hand over her mouth and a knife to her throat. The attacker shined a light in her face and told her not to scream or he would cut her throat. The attacker told her all he wanted was her money. He walked into the living room area of her apartment and never returned. Police found that the telephone and cable TV lines had been cut.

The attacker was described as a white male, 6 feet tall, who wore a ski mask, long pants, long-sleeve shirt, and gloves and carried a flashlight. The victim, who had called police several times in August with peeping-tom reports, said her attacker had a gravelly voice.

After getting some rest from his late-night activity at Erin Olson's, Bill was ready for more activity that evening. Except this time he wanted to complete his attack, so he went back to North Canton.

Patrolman Mike Grimes of the North Canton Police Department was on patrol and paying particular attention to the area of The Evergreen Trailer Park and the nearby Beckford Place Apartments due to numerous complaints of prowlers. It was about 8:30 p.m. when Grimes spotted a white male duck down into the weeds between the Evergreen Trailer Park and the apartment complex. The white male was 6 feet tall, and wore blue jeans without a shirt.

Grimes, later the North Canton police chief, alerted other units to head his way. At that exact time, police dispatchers received a complaint of a white male looking in a Beckford resident's window. He had driven off in a small blue car with Ohio license plate number 298MNB.

The officer, one block away, located the vehicle in the side lot of the apartments. The keys were in the ignition and jiggling back and forth. The engine was warm, too. The apartment manager came out and met Grimes. She said she did not recognize the car, adding it did not belong there.

Grimes ran the license plate number through NCIC. The information returned to a blue Chevy Chevette belonging to Classy Chassis on Cosmos Street in Hartville (one of Bill Griffith's automotive ventures). Two men came up to Grimes and told him they had seen the man from the Chevette looking into the window of an apartment. They had told another friend to call the police while they tried to follow the guy.

While taking statements from these witnesses, Grimes saw the shirtless man appear from the weeds and run through the trailer park. The runner eluded officers in a cat-and-mouse game until they caught him hiding behind then-London's Candies on South Main Street, three quarters of a mile south of the trailer park.

The man was 6 feet 2, had blonde hair and weighed 200 pounds, with a hairy chest and arms. He had on blue jeans with a black belt. He also had a cut on his left hand. His name was William Edward Griffith Jr. He told police he had been driving by the Beckford Apartments and some kids threw rocks at his car. So he pulled over to chase them. When he saw the police he got scared and ran.

Grimes took Griffith back to the Beckford parking lot so witnesses could see him and tell Grimes if this was the window peeper they had seen. The men could not say if this was the same guy. Grimes told them he would be forwarding a report on the incident to detectives and they would be in touch with them to look at photos. William Griffith was released, but his night was not over.

Leslie Van Housen, 16, lived on 37th Street Northeast in Canton. She was asleep on the couch in her family's living room when she woke up suddenly to see a man staring at her through the front window of her family's apartment. It was 11:30 p.m. Leslie yelled to her younger brother, who rushed into the room along with a friend.

The two juvenile boys went outside and saw the man looking in a window at a duplex across the street. They gave chase through a wooded area north into the parking lot of The Granada Apartments.

The boys saw the suspect run through the parking lot and hunch down by a set of garbage cans like he was throwing something in one of them. They could see he was wearing gloves. The man got into a small blue car parked there and fled.

Sheriff's Deputy Art Ford responded and searched the area, but could not locate anyone. He checked the garbage cans, but they were empty. In his report, Ford noted: "…Dispatch advised that North Canton Police chased a subject earlier this evening fitting the description of the peeper and the car, which was operated by William E Griffith Jr …"

Attached to Ford's report was a NCIC printout from the Miami County Sheriff's Office which requested that anyone in Ohio who experienced home break-ins and rapes of female occupants should contact them to share information.

2

January 8, 1987

Emboldened yet again by a feeling of invincibility, Bill was convinced the police were too simple-minded to put together a case against him so he pressed on with his insatiable appetite for more victims and for more sex, while in control and calling the shots.

Lt. Chip McCullough of the Lawrence Township Police Department in Stark County was on patrol at 9:36 p.m. on January 8th, when he noticed a blue Chevy Chevette with Ohio license plate number 298MNB parked at State Route 93 and Tritts Road. McCullough noted in his report that he felt the vehicle was a hazard parked there and ran the vehicle identification number to see if it was stolen. A sheriff's dispatcher heard the information and alerted McCullough that the individual was a suspect in rapes and voyeurisms around the county.

McCullough radioed for a tow truck and turned on his overhead emergency lights. The lights illuminated the area when out of the darkness appeared William E Griffith Jr. (he had a habit of doing that), wearing a gray fatigue coat and blue jeans. McCullough gave Griffith a verbal warning and sent him on his way.

November 4, 1987

Susan Park lived on Manchester Road in Canal Fulton, then a small village and now a city in Stark County. At approximately 3:30 a.m., the 33-year-old was awakened by a man who wore a ski mask. He stood over her with his hand over her mouth and pressing a knife against her throat. He told her that if she screamed he would kill her.

He ordered her to remove her underwear and spread her legs. The attacker rubbed her breasts and vagina and put his fingers inside her vagina. He then ordered Susan to masturbate while he watched. Moments later, the attacker ordered his victim to go to her children's bedroom, close the door, and stay there until daylight. He added that he was just going to take a few things.

When Lawrence Township police responded, they found the phone had been ripped from the wall and thrown into the backyard. Nothing was taken. The house was just a couple hundred feet from the intersection of Tritts and Manchester roads, where 10 months earlier Griffith's car was found parked along the road.

On Dec. 9, 1987, a Lordstown Township mother, 29, was raped in her trailer park home just south of Warren and a day before a woman, 28, living in the Randolph Acres Trailer Park in Portage County's Mogadore, was awakened by a ski-masked rapist, who fondled his victim, raped her with his fingers and forced her to perform oral sex. Both cases had many similarities to those that law enforcement agencies across Ohio had been investigating.

Then on February 18, 1988, *Janet Higgins* was just 17 and lived with her mother in Portage County's Atwater. Portage County Detective Donnie Brown was called at home at 4:20 a.m. to respond to a rape victim being treated at Robinson Memorial Hospital in nearby Ravenna. Brown arrived and spoke with Janet's mother, *Barbara,* who had been at work when her daughter's attack occurred.

Barbara told Brown that at 9:30 the night before the attack, she heard a banging noise on her enclosed patio porch. She opened the front door and heard a car rev its engine and speed away. She saw the rear lights of the vehicle as it fled and said it looked like an older model car.

Barbara told the detective she worked midnights and usually left the residence around 11:30 p.m. She returned about 8 a.m. and noted that her daughter was alone at home. Since the beginning of February, she and Janet had been experiencing an inordinate number of prank phone calls.

When the rape exam was completed, the victim told

detectives that her attacker wore a ski mask, put his hand over her mouth, and put an object against her throat. The attacker told her not to scream and that "we won't hurt you." The attacker told Janet to take off her clothes so she would not run. She complied.

He told her he would not rape her, but then had her slide back on the bed and spread her legs. Ordered to the floor, she was made to perform oral sex on him before being told to go to her mother's bedroom, where he performed oral sex on her. The attacker asked if she was a virgin and she said no. He then raped her vaginally for about two minutes before he escorted her to the bathroom, where he told her to stay for 30 minutes and not call police.

Janet waited a few minutes before leaving the bathroom. She tried to call her mother at work, but the phone was dead. The teen dressed and went to a neighbor's to call her mother.

She described her attacker as being 5 feet 10, with a "5 o'clock shadow" beard, which she felt on her thighs during the oral sex. Janet added that the rapist wore dark clothes and a dark ski mask. During the investigation, officers realized the Higgins residence was three-quarters of a mile from the residence in Rootstown Township where William E Griffith Jr. was arrested in 1981 for window peeping.

Then on April 12, less than two months after the teen-ager's rape, the straw that broke the camel's back occurred when Melissa Brown was raped in her Jackson Township home on the living room floor. Chapter 2 of this book detailed Melissa's account of the attack. A rape kit was placed in evidence along with latent tennis shoe prints.

Investigation

And

Prosecution

"These are a group of people who are the sickest of the sick. They are truly perverts and it's not curable. Instead of civil detention, we ought to make sure...these offenders... are locked up forever."

Former Florida Governor Jeb Bush

Chapter 9

It was about 5 a.m. on April 12 when the phone rang at my residence. A Jackson Township police dispatcher told me three officers were on Rob Street Northwest where a rape had been reported by a single white female. I was very familiar with the allotment and the rapes reported over the years.

I got up instantly and told the dispatcher to tell the officers at the scene to get out of the residence and secure it until I arrived. It turned out there was no need to tell officers to exit the residence because when Melissa fled to her neighbor's home the male locked Melissa's door as he removed her son from the Brown apartment.

When I arrived, an officer gave me the key and I instructed the officer to take Melissa to her hospital of choice for an exam and rape kit. Due to my recent transfer to the detective bureau, I had been to a training class where the instructor emphasized the pristine nature of a crime scene and that you only get one chance to collect evidence before it's gone forever. Instead of going inside and looking around, I decided to wait for the Stark County Crime Lab personnel to process the scene.

Crime Lab Director Bob Budgake and Criminalist Michelle Mitchell arrived about an hour after I did and I briefed them on what we knew. I showed them how you could stand in the backyard of the residence and look at the roof and see a bent-up screen. Also, I had gotten a ladder from a neighbor and looked closer at the roof, where I found the receiver of Melissa's kitchen phone in the gutter. I touched nothing until lab personnel arrived.

Bob wanted to go in and look at the scene before bringing in their equipment, so I unlocked the back door that led to the kitchen. I was just about to take a step inside when Bob said, "Wow, look at those shoe prints!" I stepped back and asked him, "Where are you looking? I don't see anything." Budgake pointed and bent over. "Right there, the oblique light enables you to see them."

At that point, I knew I needed to get out of their way and stay out. "Bob, I can't see a thing. I better stay outside and you two go in and take care of it," I said. Bob walked in, with Michelle following behind. They invited me to follow behind Michelle. Part way into the kitchen, Bob took two kitchen chairs and placed them over the area of the shoe prints in order to protect them from bumbling detectives.

In the living room I saw a pillow lying on the floor in front of the TV. Next to the pillow was a small jar of Vaseline. At that point I told Bob and Michelle I was going outside to take photographs. Bob and Michelle spent the better part of their workday processing the scene. It was a sight to behold.

Bob processed the kitchen area. He used his fingerprint dusting kit like Da Vinci used his paints, brushing the dark contrasting powder with even, fluid strokes. Bob intently paid attention to detail, deep in concentration all the while he watched and waited for a pattern to rise up from the color and shapes of his work, like Da Vinci with his canvas. Slowly a glimmer, a shadowy image began to emerge from Bob's canvas, the linoleum floor. There it was a beautiful defined outline of a tennis shoe. Bob's masterpiece was complete!

He had black fingerprint powder EVERYWHERE! To my amazement, slowly but surely, Budgake raised tennis shoe prints that depicted an individual walking out the back door. The prints were very clear now.

The apartment was a total mess from fingerprint powder on the floor, the window sill of the child's bedroom where entry had been gained and the door frames in the other rooms in the apartment. The way it looked I thought the landlord would never be able to rent this place again. Before the Crime Lab personnel left, they had lifted a partial tennis shoe print from the window sill in the boy's bedroom as well as three latent shoe prints with the same pattern from the kitchen floor.

There were four latent fingerprint lifts taken from various locations in the apartment, latent lifts of fabric impressions from gloves, vacuum contents from the carpeted area where the rape took place, the bed sheets, a pry mark from the kitchen door and the mangled screen from the roof along with the phone receiver and countless photographs.

At the hospital, Melissa Brown had completed the long procedure and examination for the rape kit. Officers at the hospital were able to bring the kit back to Bob and Michelle who took it to the lab. They were extremely thorough.

I met Melissa at the police department and took a taped statement from her in which she detailed her account of the attack. Melissa made a point about the attacker's odor. "It's like when you walk into a mechanic's garage or a gas station. It was an oily and greasy smell like he was a mechanic." She also said her attacker was physically fit with strong forearms and broad shoulders. He was 6 feet tall, weighed 190 pounds and was probably in his late 20s to early 30s. Melissa added that he could not maintain an erection.

After Melissa left my office with her parents and son, I got a message from the rental company for Frances Acres. The woman in the office told me that she had received a phone call from a *Barbara Norris* on Portage Street Northwest about loud noises she had heard at about 4:30 that morning. Jackson Detective Bob Notman and I went to Norris's home and interviewed her at 8:30 p.m.

Norris said she had trouble sleeping and had been lying on her couch when she heard her neighbor's screen door slam. About five minutes later she heard a loud banging noise, as if someone had thrown something at her shed or gutter. She said she got up and looked out the window, but did not see anyone and went back to bed.

Notman and I then did a door-to-door canvass of the neighborhood to see if anyone else saw or heard anything. We spoke with *Rachel Mimms,* who lived two doors east of Melissa Brown. She said she could not sleep the prior evening and at 2:30 a.m. got a hardboiled egg from the refrigerator. She ate it while gazing out the back window and looking at the blackness of the night.

Her only light was from her stove-top range. She said she was startled by a white male who walked past her carport in a westerly direction at a quick pace. In a moment he was gone. To the best of her recollection, he was 5 feet 7 to 6 feet tall and wore all dark clothing. Rachel showed us the area where she witnessed the man walking. We also noticed a light from a large mercury vapor lamp from the middle of the field between the apartment units on Portage and Rob streets.

Notman and I were able to locate another Rob Street resident, *Karen Reese,* who lived further east of Rachel. Karen said that earlier that day one of her neighbors told her about the attack. She said that she noticed a large step stool that she kept in her carport was now missing. When she described it, I immediately remembered seeing one like it earlier that morning in the carport of Melissa Brown's unit. The attacker must have parked his vehicle somewhere to the east of Brown's residence and walked behind the Rob Street apartment units to conceal himself. He picked up the stool to help boost him into the bedroom window of Melissa's son.

No other tenants recalled hearing or seeing anything else the morning of the attack.

In the days that followed I began to review case files from prior rapes in the allotment. As the weeks passed, I spoke with other investigators from Jackson who had worked on those cases. I located old suspects they had developed in order to determine their whereabouts when Melissa's attack occurred. I ran down people who worked for the rental company as well as garbage men, postal carriers, cable installers, personnel from utility companies – you name it. They all were checked out. No concrete suspects were developed.

Dennis Florea was a Canton police officer assigned to the Stark County Crime Lab. Among his many tasks, Dennis analyzed impression evidence and latent prints. Within a week of the attack on Melissa Brown, Florea phoned me about the latent lifts of the tennis shoe prints. I went to the lab where Dennis gave me a photocopy of the best print Budgake and Mitchell lifted. Florea said he had been busy going to different shoe and sporting goods stores in an attempt to locate what type of shoe left the impressions.

Florea said the key to this type of evidence is to locate and secure the shoes before the wear pattern changes. He hoped that the attacker did not wear the shoes every day. If he did, there was only a short time to get the shoes or the prints would be useless. He also said that if I could find the shoes without the wear pattern changed, they could be just as valuable as a fingerprint for identification purposes.

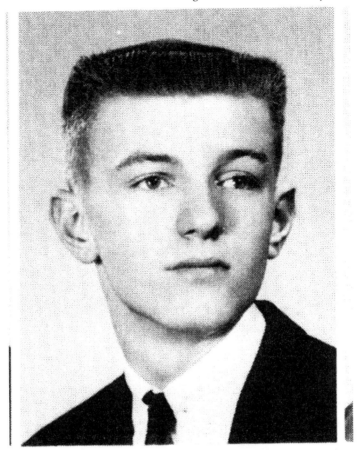

William Griffith

GRIFFITH, WILLIAM E.   **Stroker**
Sr. Farewell Committee; Career Day Rep. Hi-Y. **Preferences:** Fast, Blue
'59 Impalas, Family, Lynn, Police Car 9.

1999 Picture of Griffith in prison

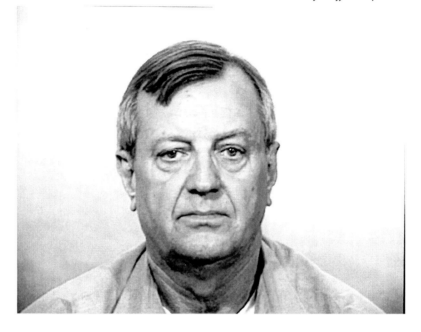

1993 Picture of Griffith taken by
Portage County Sheriff at prison interviewed for rape

William E. Griffith Jr.
Dob. 11-06-42

1983 Booking photo for voyeurism by Lawrence Twp. P.D.

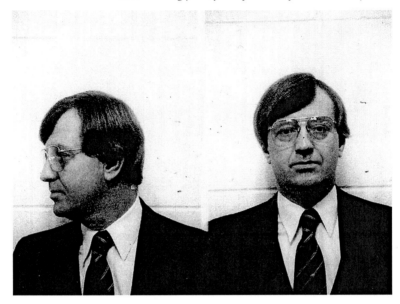

1988 Booking photo for Rape by Jackson Township Police.

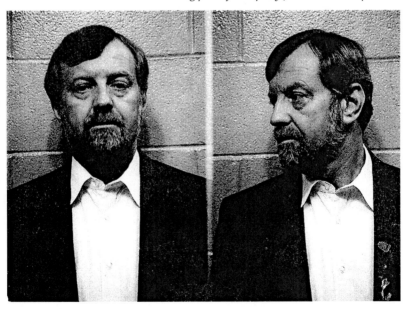

These pictures were taken at the Tulsa, Oklahoma airport by a Beckham County Sheriff detective in May 1988. For the first time in Bill Griffith's life he was no longer the hunter, he was now the hunted.

April 1988 photo of front of Melissa Brown's residence

View of rear and west side of Brown residence showing son's bedroom windows

Rear view of Melissa Brown's residence

View from roof of Brown residence toward backyard

Mangled screen from son's bedroom window on Brown's roof.

Weather stripping from son's window on Brown roof

Telephone receiver from kitchen phone in gutter on Brown roof

Pry marks from window in Brown kitchen.

Pry marks on window of Brown's son's bedroom window.

Latent prints on door jam of kitchen door exiting residence.

Naked eye view of shoe print on son's bedroom window sill.

Naked eye view of shoe print on son's bedroom window sill with ruler.

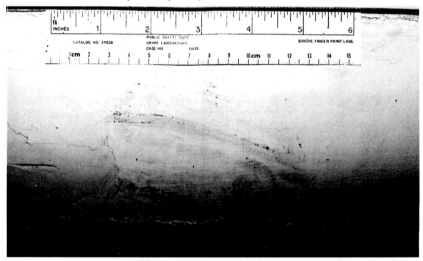

Detective Rudy in kitchen of Brown residence.

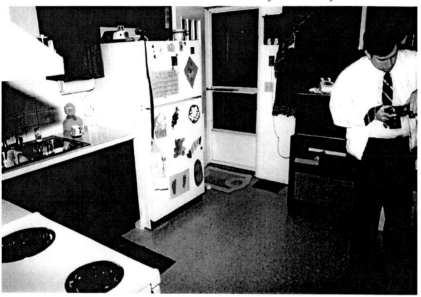

View from entrance into kitchen of Brown residence.

Steak knife used to threaten Melissa Brown left in the kitchen sink after attack.

View from front door of living room floor where rape occurred (pillow and Vaseline)

View from kitchen of living room floor where rape occurred.

View from living room down the hallway toward victim's bedroom.

Melissa Brown's son's bedroom.

Melissa Brown's bedroom.

Kitchen floor covered with fingerprint powder.

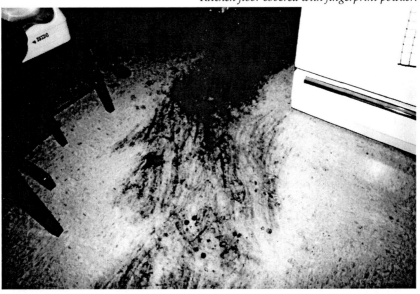

Kitchen floor with powder revealing latent shoe prints.

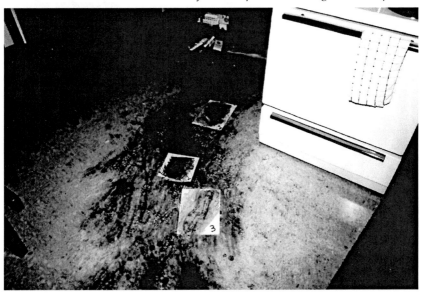

Griffith tennis shoe used for comparison linking him to Melissa Brown rape.

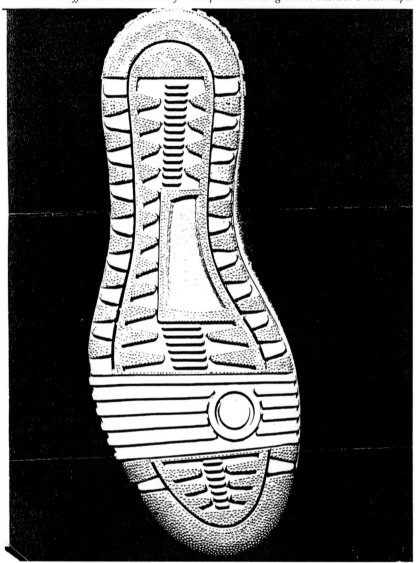

*"Most commonly, rape is a crime of opportunity; the
victim is chosen not because of her looks or behavior,
but because she is there."*

From Virgin or Vamp: How the Press Covers Sex Crimes
by Helen Benedict, Oxford University Press, 1992.

Chapter 10

One day in early May 1988, I testified before the Stark
County grand jury and then went to the county courthouse
annex, where the prosecutor's office was located. An
investigator had an office there. His name was Tom Kell,
whom I considered the most knowledgeable investigator in
Stark County at that time. Kell always had time to talk to you
and would give you advice (if you wanted it), and would
point you in the right direction. I always enjoyed spending
time talking with him. I tried to be a sponge around Kell and
soak up whatever knowledge I could.

When I told Tom about the investigation, he told me
about similar investigations over the years and that there had
been some suspects developed. He said the incident I was
investigating fit with what other detectives had looked into
countless times over the past decade.   Kell told me that the
investigative unit he had worked with only had a couple of
investigators still assigned to it, but he felt sure that I could
get whatever information they had.

The Canton-Stark County Criminal Investigation Unit
had shrunk to only Detective Tim Swanson and half a dozen
Canton City Police Detectives. Kell had retired and went to
work for the Stark County Prosecutor's Office. Detectives
working on the past rape cases had developed these similar
points: an odor from the attacker, which varied from a
medical type of hand wash to an oily, gasoline-type smell; a

steak knife from the victim's kitchen was often used as the weapon; and the attacker also had a difficult time maintaining an erection during the assaults.

Kell asked if I knew Stark County Sheriff's Detective Tim Swanson. I told him I had never met Swanson. Kell picked up the phone and called Swanson and told him about the investigation. Swanson had kept all the files that had been developed about the rape cases. Swanson said he would see me, if I came over to his office.

At that time, a yellow rock-like substance had flooded Stark County from Detroit, Michigan. It was the introduction of crack cocaine, and it became an epidemic. Those working with the Canton-Stark County Criminal Intelligence Unit, along with the Stark County Metropolitan Narcotics Unit, were busy educating themselves and everyone else in county law enforcement about crack cocaine and the related criminal issues it raised. The area was under siege from a loosely knit gang of black youths referred to as "The Detroit Boys." They were making a fortune away from Detroit in a new market while causing enormous problems in Stark County. While everyone was concentrated on those issues, the rape investigations had been put on the back burner.

I met Swanson and briefed him about the Melissa Brown case. As I talked, Swanson got up from his desk and opened a tall metal filing cabinet and brought out a couple of large accordion-style folders and charts. He told me this was the work product of years of gathering information about the county's Ski Mask Rapist. He added that the incident I had begun to work on was the same as all the others.

Swanson said three suspects had been developed from the work efforts of the Canton-Stark Criminal Intelligence Unit. The best suspect was a man from Hartville named William Griffith Jr. Swanson said they had watched him for weeks, but could not catch him doing anything, let alone anything illegal. As time went on, they had to move on to other cases. Swanson told me I was free to look at, read, copy or use whatever I needed from those files. Swanson also said that he would provide assistance, if he had the time, but that his unit was busy with the crack cocaine problem.

Over the next few months I became a fixture at that office. I read through the voluminous files Swanson had maintained and educated myself on the history of the rapes in Stark and neighboring counties, and the history of the formation of the criminal intelligence unit which tried to assimilate information to identify the attacker.

At that point in time, Stark County law enforcement was not working together. Each police department worked their own rape cases. However, detectives did talk with one another and exchanged information and hunches on what they thought was going on and who was responsible. For the sake of space, I have listed only those rapes that had a similar modus operandi. Keep in mind, there were other rapes reported in Stark County.

The Criminal Intelligence Unit was created because of a 1983 case when Jack Hanley was convicted of an arson fire at his restaurant, The Red Lantern, located in Jackson Township.

Hanley did a year in federal prison in Springfield, Missouri. While incarcerated, Hanley gave information to FBI agents in Canton about corruption inside Canton City Hall.

Agents from the local FBI field office brought Hanley back to Canton and asked area police chiefs to form a cooperative unit comprised of detectives from local police agencies in Stark County in order to do a sweeping investigation. The unit was called the Canton-Stark County Criminal Intelligence Unit.

The corruption case was investigated simultaneously with hundreds of unsolved residential burglaries. Stark County law enforcement had more than enough on its plate investigating illegal activity without considering rape investigations.

Eventually, three government officials were charged and convicted as a result of the corruption case and one man was charged with numerous burglaries and fencing stolen property. While all of these investigations were proceeding, Canton Police Detective John Kotagides took his concerns about the numerous rapes to Detective Tom Kell, who had been the representative for the Canton Police Department on the Criminal Intelligence Unit.

Stark County Prosecutor James Unger tasked detectives with developing a suspect who could be responsible for all of the ski-mask attacks. Their first order of business was to have the FBI take a look at the cases and provide them with an "offender profile." The following is the actual criminal personality profile provided by the psychological profiler for the FBI's Cleveland Field Division in 1982.

It should be noted that this profile is based on probabilities, and any suspect developed may or may not fit in each and every category.

Victimology

The information provided is somewhat limited because of the nature of the flow chart. It appears that most of the victims reside in the same geographical area; i.e., North Canton. Probably the victim did not know the subject, but he knew her.

Modus Operandi and Crime Scene Analysis

This subject typically will attack between the hours of midnight and 5 a.m., in a residence or a residential area. He picks a victim who is alone or has small children, and selects them by peeping. The subject is typically on foot.

The aggression will increase slightly from case to case over time, and he will usually use a weapon of opportunity. There will be a short time period for the crime. It will be a single assault, and he will continue until caught.

The subject may call the victim prior to and after the attack. He will ask the victim to remove clothing and just expose the area of attack. The subject will experience premature ejaculation or impotence. He will use only enough force to overtake victim. He uses little or no profanity and will demand some verbal activity with the victim. He will do only what she will allow him to do. If resisted, he will negotiate, stop, flee or threaten. He may apologize after the crime, might take a souvenir, and may keep a diary.

Offender Profile

This attacker will be single, white; his age will be plus or minus three years of the victim. The subject may misjudge the age of some victims if they do not look their age. He will be an inadequate personality; an under-achiever; gentle and passive; have a high school education or less; if a veteran, he received a general discharge. He will collect pornography; he is non-athletic; is a peeper; if he has a criminal background it will be for breaking and entering; voyeurism and peeping. His residence will be nearby; and if living with parents, his mother will be dominant.

He will be a "loner" with few friends. If he dates, it will be with a significantly younger girl. He is a nocturnal person who frequents adult bookstores and movies. He has a menial job with little or no public contact. He is not a messy dresser.

Interview Techniques

Talk to ex-wife if he has one

Interview away from Police Department; i.e.,

Motel room, etc.

Night interview

Non-attacking

Counselor approach

Say you understood his feelings

In the early and mid-1980's, there was not a lot of coordination between local and national agencies. The FBI's VICAP (Violent Criminal Apprehension Program) was being formulated by Los Angeles Police Homicide Detective Pierce Brooks and FBI Special Agent Robert Ressler. In 1985, VICAP became a reality and was located at the FBI training academy in Quantico, Virginia. It provided a national clearinghouse of information to assist investigators by tracking and correlating violent crime, especially murder. Sexual assaults were soon included in the late 1980's. Prior to VICAP's establishment, police departments were only as good at sharing and coordinating this type of information as the individual investigator who was assigned to that particular investigation. In Stark County in the 1980's there was not a lot of sharing or coordinating of intelligence. There was/is a turf protection mentality throughout the area. The community suffered because of it.

As I continued to read and educate myself about Bill Griffith, I learned that Griffith had been arrested twice in the early 1980's and ordered to undergo psychological counseling for his voyeurism problem. No one had any idea the problem was much deeper than mere window peeping.

On April 29, 1981, Portage County Sheriff's deputies

had arrested Bill and taken his fingerprints and a photograph. It was the first time Bill appeared on the radar of law enforcement since he was shot in Akron in 1968 while peeping, and the first time he was arrested since 1964 in Ypsilanti, Michigan.

In 1981, *Donald Prather* lived in a duplex on State Route 44 in Portage County's small bucolic Rootstown. He shared the duplex structure with a neighbor to the east, Portage County sheriff's deputy Bob Burgess. At approximately 9:45 p.m. on Friday night, April 29th, Prather and his wife were entertaining friends at their home.

The guests were ready to leave and getting into their car when Prather and his wife noticed a white male at the corner of the neighboring duplex to the west. He was wearing a light gray suit and tie while peeping in the front window. The resident there was a single female who lived alone. Prather told his wife to call Deputy Burgess to see if he was home.

Prather watched from his garage as the man peeping in the window had his hand in his pants, apparently playing with himself. Prather went inside to put on a pair of shoes, and his wife told him that Burgess was getting ready to come over to help. Prather went back out and saw the man still standing at his neighbor's window, with his penis in his hand, openly masturbating.

As Prather started toward Burgess's house to see what was taking Burgess so long he peered back over his shoulder and saw the peeper walking down the driveway toward State Route 44. Prather called to Burgess to hurry and jumped in his car. Burgess ran to Prather's car, jumped in the passenger side, and noticed the unidentified man now running full tilt toward a dark-colored station wagon parked on the highway. The station wagon had Pennsylvania license plates. Burgess recorded the number and told Prather to follow the car at a normal distance.

Burgess explained to Prather that his wife had called the sheriff's office to let them know what was going on and to send a cruiser in the direction of his house. Prather followed the station wagon until they came to a traffic light at State Route 224. Burgess instructed Prather to pull up alongside the station wagon when the driver got out. That driver walked behind the station wagon to check out the luggage carrier he had affixed to the top of his car.

The unidentified man looked at Burgess and asked him, "Do you have a problem?" Burgess replied, "No, do you?" The man replied, "Yeah, my luggage carrier came off my roof and I had to stop and pick it up back there in someone's yard on Route 44." At this point Deputy D.B. Simon pulled up in his cruiser in the parking lot of the nearby T&O restaurant.

The man in the gray suit and tie was identified as William E. Griffith Jr. from Cosmos Street in Hartville Ohio. Griffith explained to the deputy what he was doing when Burgess pulled Deputy Simon aside. Together they examined the white luggage carrier on top of Griffith's vehicle. The luggage carrier had no abrasions or marks on it to indicate it had fallen off the vehicle. Simon spoke briefly with Prather about what Prather had witnessed and then placed Griffith under arrest for voyeurism and criminal trespass.

The suspect was taken to the Portage County jail where he was fingerprinted for the first time in Ohio, photographed, and placed in a jail cell. Griffith's paperwork at the county jail listed him as 6 feet 2 inches tall and 190 pounds. His eyes were blue and his hair was blonde. A couple of hours later, Griffith's bond was posted by a bail bond company. Griffith later appeared in Ravenna Municipal Court, pled guilty to the charges, and was ordered to obtain counseling for his admitted voyeurism problem.

The bond paperwork revealed Griffith was a salesman of medical supplies. Bill had switched from selling insurance to pharmaceuticals. Bill still was given a car by his employer and was out on the open road.

Griffith soon began counseling for his voyeurism issues at The Emerge Ministries on Mull Avenue in Akron with Dr. Daniel Brooks, but had not exactly thrown himself into rehabilitation for his problem. He had to go to counseling as part of his court sentence and to show Marilyn he was sincere about getting help. However, Bill was smarter than everyone else; he would go through the motions and continue to feed his desires. Besides, no one knew what he knew. They had no idea.

The other documented arrest of Bill Griffith took place after an incident on September 28, 1983. *Jack Danforth* was the manager of Forty Corner's trailer park at the corner of State Route 21 and Forty Corners Street in Lawrence Township north of Massillon. At 10 p.m., he walked out of his trailer and noticed a man walking between trailers located near his own trailer. The man appeared to be peeping in the windows.

Danforth soon noticed two other residents he knew walking down Thomas Boulevard by Nicholas Circle. Danforth walked up to *Carl Nix* and *Sam Jackson* and asked them what they were doing. The men told him that Jackson's wife told them that a man was looking at her through her bedroom window.

Danforth told the men he was going to call Lawrence Township Police. After he did so, Danforth came back outside and saw a few men chasing an unknown person across State Route 21 and disappeared into the darkness.

When Lawrence Police Lt. Chip McCullough arrived, he was led to Thomas Boulevard where residents had discovered a suspicious vehicle believed to be connected to the peeper. McCullough ran the license plate number on the 1981 blue Chevy Impala station wagon and it returned to Wheels Inc. of Cosmos Street in Hartville. McCullough had the vehicle towed and inventoried. The inventory included a wallet in the glove box that contained a driver's license and credit cards that belonged to William E Griffith Jr. of Cosmos Street in Hartville. An alert dispatcher at the Stark County Sheriff's Office radioed Lt. McCullough and advised him that Griffith could be related to the rapes and voyeurisms that were plaguing the county.

McCullough had Uniontown Police go to the Cosmos address and speak to Marilyn Griffith. She told the police her husband was out of town on business and that he had reported his license as lost over a year ago. Over the next week, McCullough completed an investigation and charged William Griffith with voyeurism. Bill was fingerprinted and photographed at the Massillon City Jail and pled guilty to one count of voyeurism. Massillon Municipal Judge Richard T. Kettler ordered Griffith to get counseling.

As noted earlier, Bill had been attending counseling sessions at The Emerge Ministries in Akron with Dr. Daniel Brooks since his arrest in Portage County in 1981; however, Dr. Brooks was moving to Missouri and could no longer counsel Griffith. Marilyn Griffith was very distraught with the second arrest of her husband and spoke to her minister at The Bethel Temple, her church in Canton. Dr. Brooks and the minister from The Bethel Temple asked *Dr. Dean Edwards* to take Bill Griffith as a special case.

As a rule Edwards does not get involved in counseling criminal defendants because of the complications arising from depositions and trials. However, on this occasion he agreed to see Bill as a favor to his pastor. Edwards told me in a 2009 interview that he never had any indication from Griffith that Griffith was involved in rape. Edwards counseled Griffith as a voyeur.

According to Edwards, Griffith's son, Robert, was devastated by his father's arrest and criminal activity. His wife Marilyn was in total shock and had no idea that her husband was a voyeur. To think that the police could suspect

Bill of raping dozens of women was totally incomprehensible to her. Most women get an idea that something strange is going on with their husband when they are involved in voyeuristic activity. Not Marilyn. She was very fearful of things that she did not know or understand and she was very fearful of Bill and his family.

In the opinion of Dr. Edwards, everyone has a little voyeur in them. This is what makes gossip and scandal so intriguing. However, most of us have a well-developed conscience that keeps us from crossing the boundaries of fantasy into the reality of illicit activity. Others, like Bill, do not know how to deal with the stresses of daily life, so they develop ways of acting out to relieve the tensions.

While most of us develop the necessary mental, intellectual, emotional and spiritual skills to release this tension, people like Bill allow the line between fantasy and reality to become blurred and resort to voyeurism as a way of relieving the tension through sexual excitement.

After a time, however, voyeuristic activity no longer was stimulating enough for Bill to reach orgasm, so he took the next step…rape. Bill mentally compartmentalized this activity and denied to himself that it ever happened. He disassociated himself from the activity, which allowed him to function and appear as a normal person in society during the day and no one was the wiser.

According to Dr. Edwards, most voyeurs never rape. However, Bill had accumulated so much stress and his sexual urges became so compelling that voyeuristic fantasy was no longer compelling enough to help him reach orgasm. Bill did not hurt his victims through physical beatings or graduate to killing because he knew what he was doing was wrong. Bill's pattern was due to his compelling compulsion to continue. He did not have a healthy conscience, and the compelling nature of his sexual urges overrode what conscience he did have.

Dr. Edwards further explained that everyone has evil urges, fantasies and ideas, but we have a conscience that is strong enough to inhibit us from carrying them out. Bill's conscience, however, was not strong enough to stop his will. Edwards stated that Bill had uncanny ways of concealing his activities from his wife, family and even from his counselor. This was evidenced by his committing so many rapes over such a long period of time without being caught.

Swanson told me that he strongly suspected that Bill Griffith was the rapist everyone was trying to identify because of an interview he conducted with Griffith and his attorney in 1986. The interview had been arranged after Griffith was picked up as a suspect in two voyeurism incidents at two Stark County locations on August 20, 1986, which I detailed in Chapter 8.

Detective Swanson's interview report noted that Griffith answered only general questions on the advice of his attorney. Swanson also noted Griffith was very nervous during the interview, but answered all questions regarding his background. Swanson also paid attention to Griffith's grooming and odors. Griffith verified his military service, his arrest for disorderly conduct and voyeurism by Michigan State Police in December 1964, and the name of his first wife. Griffith also confirmed he had received counseling at Emerge Ministries in Akron by Dr. Dean Edwards for voyeurism problems. Griffith also said that he did not drink or smoke. He added that he was active at his church, The Bethel Temple in Canton, taught Sunday school and helped with the youth group.

On September 11, 1986, Swanson telephoned Teresa Martin, Bill Griffith's first wife. She confirmed her earlier marriage to Bill and that they had a daughter. She added that Griffith had never met his daughter and had no contact with her. Teresa also told Swanson that Griffith had reportedly been shot in Akron 20 years earlier, apparently after peeping in someone's windows.

In a 2009 interview with co-author Davis, Stark County Sheriff Timothy W. Swanson said that when he interviewed William Griffith in 1986 he was convinced that Griffith was the Stark County ski-mask rapist, but he did not have the evidence to file charges.

> *"Rape is something the victim will never forget…It's not fair
> (to have time limits on prosecution)…Going through the court
> process and seeing the rapist
> put away can restore the victim's sense of power."*

Kathleen Trissel, Director American Red Cross Rape Crisis Program in Canton
Akron Beacon Journal, August 21, 1988

Chapter 11

Reading about numerous rape cases and the activities of William E Griffith Jr., I decided to run a check on Griffith's driving record. That check revealed 12 traffic citations for moving violations issued from 1979 through 1986. More interesting were the eight different counties in which the citations were written – Stark, Summit, Cuyahoga, Portage, Richland, Medina, Licking and Franklin. He had been virtually all over the state.

On May 21, 1988, *Eric Jensen* of Daytona Avenue Northwest in Jackson Township was going to let his dog out the front door of his duplex at 10:20 p.m. Jensen immediately noticed a man standing at the sliding glass doors of his neighbor's duplex. The neighbor's unit faced Bermuda Avenue Northwest. The unidentified man tugged on the door in an apparent attempt to get inside. Jensen went inside his duplex to call the Jackson Township police.

Afterward, Jensen went back outside and saw that the suspect had moved down the block to the rear of a duplex on Ocala Avenue Northwest. The man stopped and looked in an illuminated window where there appeared to be a woman in the room. He then walked over to a blue Oldsmobile station wagon that had an Ohio license plate with the number 142HSD. The vehicle had numerous cardboard boxes in the back seat. He then drove north on Ocala Avenue with his lights off. The lights on the vehicle were turned on when the man reached the intersection of Ocala and Daytona and left the allotment of duplexes.

Jensen described the man as a white male, 6 feet 2 inches tall, who weighed approximately 190 pounds, and wore blue jeans and a blue sweatshirt with the word M-I-C-H-I-G-A-N spelled out in white block letters on the chest. Jensen also said the man had an athletic build.

A Jackson Township police cruiser arrived within one minute. As Jensen told the officer about his observations, a call came over the police radio advising officers to be on the lookout for a white male whose description resembled the one Jensen had just phoned in about the Daytona suspect. A man fitting the same description had just been observed peeping in the window of a woman on Hills and Dales Road Northwest while she was washing dishes. The woman screamed and the man ran from the scene.

The officer left Jensen and went to the Hills and Dales Road site. He determined that the descriptions were identical right down to the sweatshirt with white block letters. It developed that the license plate of the blue Oldsmobile station wagon was registered to Wheels Incorporated located at the same 17th Street Northeast address in Canton where the parents of Bill Griffith lived. I was not advised of these incidents for two days.

Within days after reading numerous accounts of rape incidents throughout Stark County, I learned that no one had ever approached a Griffith family member to determine what he or she might know. I figured it was worth a shot and went to the residence of Griffith's parents in Canton on May 24th, 1988. Detective Bob Notman also went along.

I went into shock when we pulled up to the Griffith home. Right across the street from the Griffith house was the Stark County Battered Woman's Shelter. The shelter served as a "safe house" for victims of domestic violence who needed refuge from a violent predator. "You could have knocked me over with a feather," I told Notman. "If this ain't the fox guarding the hen house I don't know what is." The primary suspect was right across the street from so many potential victims.

Griffith's mother, Maudie, met us at the front door. Notman was closer to her in age and began to explain our reason for being there. While they spoke, I noticed a huge pile of clothing in the dining room off the foyer entrance to the house. Maudie said the clothes belonged to her son, Bill, who was staying with them. She told us he traveled a lot with his new job. She also said he was having marital problems with his wife, Marilyn, and that they were separated. Maudie told us that she did not want to speak to us without her husband being present. She would give him our business cards when he came home from work and was sure he would call. When we left the house I told Notman that I saw some tennis shoes on the dining room floor.

That evening, Notman had other commitments so I went to the Canton PD and spoke with John Boerner, a detective I knew. Since the talk with Griffith's father would be later in the evening, I wanted to talk to William Griffith Sr. at the Canton detective bureau rather than make Griffith Sr. drive out to my office in Jackson Township.

William Griffith Sr. called me and said he could meet about 8:30 p.m. At 8:30 sharp, Griffith Sr. strolled into the detective bureau and met with Detective Boerner and me. Boerner had been around for years and was familiar with the rape investigations that potentially involved Griffith's son.

We went into one of the detective interview rooms and asked Griffith Sr. if he was aware of any problems with his son and his prior arrests for voyeurism.

At first, Mr. Griffith thought we had wanted to talk to

him about the car business his son had been operating, which was called "Griffith and Sons." He said he had received angry calls in the past from dissatisfied people and he did not want to get in the middle of that. Griffith acknowledged that his son had some issues with voyeurism, but he did not believe they were serious and his son was receiving counseling. He said his son was living with his parents because Bill was having problems with his wife, Marilyn. Mr. Griffith claimed Marilyn was intolerable.

He also said his son was currently working for a pollution cleanup company headquartered in Oklahoma City, Oklahoma. His son was tired of all the travel and wanted to move his family out there, but his wife was a big problem. We asked Mr. Griffith when his son was last home and stayed with him. Bill had been home the prior weekend. I asked Mr. Griffith what his son used for transportation when he was in town, Griffith said that he allowed his son to use his car or the truck from Griffith and Sons that was at his house on 17th Street.

The truck he referred to was the flatbed tow truck Griffith used to pick up wrecked vehicles before refurbishing them. I asked Griffith if he let his son use his blue station wagon on May 21st. Mr. Griffith responded that he had let Bill use the car so he could visit his children in Hartville. I finally told William Sr. that I felt his son's problem had progressed to more than just window peeping and that he had graduated to raping the women he was watching.

William Sr. stared at me with complete and utter contempt. He said there was no way his son was involved in anything like that and that I was mistaken. The conversation went on for awhile longer. As he left the detective bureau that evening, it was obvious that Mr. Griffith would not be assisting the police in the future.

On May 25th, I received a phone call from Detective Boerner, who said that after the interview with William

Griffith Sr. he had sent a teletype via the National Criminal Information Computer (commonly known as NCIC) to Oklahoma state law enforcement personnel. In the teletype, Boerner had included the ski-mask rapist's M.O. for the numerous unsolved rapes. He requested that if any jurisdiction had any similar crimes within the past year that they contact the Jackson Township Police or Canton Police.

He soon received two replies. One attack was more than a year old, but the other had just occurred on May 18th, just one week earlier, in Sayre, Oklahoma. The relevant Oklahoma agency was the Beckham County Sheriff's Office. Deputy Dan Marshall was the contact person for all inquiries.

I called Marshall, who related the circumstances of the case. At 1:30 a.m. on May 18th, an unknown white male who wore a ski mask cut the screen of a residence to gain entry. The attacker threatened to tie up the female, if she did not comply. Then he ordered her to get on her knees. The attacker tried to penetrate the female vaginally from behind but could not. He then had her lie on her back and spread her legs while he performed fellatio on her. He then had her get back on her knees and he entered her vagina from behind. The attacker told the female to lie still until he and his partner left. No one else was seen, and the female's small children were unharmed and asleep in their bedroom. The female woke them and took them with her to a neighbor's residence where she notified the police because she had no telephone. The female's husband worked the midnight shift.

I then filled in Deputy Marshall on what I knew of William E Griffith Jr. I also told Marshall where Griffith worked in Oklahoma City. Marshall said he would contact the employer to see if they could tell him where Griffith might have been traveling at that time.

I asked Marshall to go to the airport in Oklahoma City that evening because I knew Griffith was supposed to be returning to Oklahoma. I wanted an up-to-date photo of the suspect. The last one on file was from the arrest in 1983. I told Deputy Marshall that I had to show a photo line-up for a recent voyeurism case in which Griffith was a suspect. Marshall said he would try and would let me know the following week if he was successful.

On May 27th, I contacted Eric Jensen after his return from a business trip. I decided to use the old photo of Griffith and could not wait to see if Deputy Marshall was successful in obtaining a new one. I could not let too much time elapse as I needed to have Jensen view a photo line-up and positively identify, if possible, William E Griffith Jr. as the person he saw wearing the Michigan sweatshirt peeping in windows six days earlier. Jensen picked out the photo of Griffith without hesitation.

I contacted Massillon Municipal Court prosecutors and presented the information I had gathered to obtain arrest warrants charging William E. Griffith Jr. with three counts of voyeurism. The warrants were approved and I had them entered into NCIC so that anyone who ran any type of check on Griffith, would know that he was wanted by Jackson Township Police.

I also called Bill Griffith's employer, USPCI of Oklahoma, in an attempt to determine his travel itinerary. The human resources director said that Griffith was returning within the week because he was being let go. The human resource director also said there had been many irregularities in Griffith's Citicorp/DINERS CLUB travel account. The director assured me that the firm would comply with all subpoenas or court orders they might receive.

Jackson Township Police Chief Philip W. Paar contacted local media outlets about the arrest warrants for William Griffith. The police department began receiving telephone calls from all over the county about where Griffith was located.

One call in particular was interesting. *Betty* Silway, who lived on Hills and Dales Road, was the lady who, over a week ago, had been washing her dishes and had seen Griffith watching outside her kitchen window. Betty told me that she read about Griffith in the newspaper and remembered an incident her neighbor had told her about back in the fall of 1987. I went to Silway's residence and met her neighbor.

The neighbor told me about suspicious activity several months earlier. She awoke early one morning because of a loud banging noise and tried to phone police. She discovered that her phone line was dead. She turned on the lights and found nothing was wrong. When her husband came home from work later that day he found the phone lines had been cut outside. The phone company repaired the lines, but two weeks later the same thing happened. When the phone company came out the second time, repairmen installed a protective metal cover over the phone lines so they could not be cut. They assumed the problem was probably due to neighborhood juveniles.

On June 1st, I received a phone call from Detective Mike Smith of the Fairlawn Police Department just west of Akron. Detective Smith had seen a teletype I had sent out in May about the rapes and M.O. of the attacker. Smith mentioned several incidents in his jurisdiction that occurred in 1985, which he believed were similar. This was the first time authorities in Stark County knew about a link between the attacker and the same kind of crimes in Summit County. Arrangements were made to exchange information.

That same day, Deputy Marshall of the Beckham County Sheriff's Office notified me that he had met with Bill Griffith at the Tulsa airport on Saturday evening. He said Griffith was supposed to land in Oklahoma City, but the plane had been rerouted to Tulsa. When Marshall caught up with Griffith, he found Griffith was compliant and calm. Griffith allowed Marshall to take a couple of Polaroid photos, which the deputy then mailed to me. Griffith also agreed to answer any questions Marshall had regarding the rape in Sayre. Marshall followed up on Griffith's alibis and none of them checked out.

On June 3rd, Bill Griffith checked into the Golden Valley Health Center in Golden Valley, Minnesota. He was admitted for a psychosexual disorder and major depression and placed in the sexual dependency unit. He was accompanied by his parents, who were the only people who knew Griffith had gone there. For the first time in his life, William E. Griffith Jr. no longer was the "hunter." He was the "hunted."

Three days later, Jackson Detective Mark Machan and I met with Robert Griffith and his fiancée. Robert was the eldest son of Bill Griffith. He had called earlier and wanted to speak to me about his recent contact with his father and to help in any way possible with the investigation. Robert said that he and his fiancée had cleaned out the Griffith & Sons tow truck around April 9, 1988, and found a dark-colored ski mask and a large screwdriver. Robert's grandfather had called him on May 24th and said that he wanted to take him to see his father because his father had a legal problem. Robert met his father at a motel on South Arlington Road in Summit County. Robert asked his father if there was any truth to newspaper stories that claimed he was a rapist. He said his father shook his head in the affirmative. Robert said his grandfather told him to keep his mouth shut and not to tell the police. However, after reading local newspaper stories, Robert felt that his information could help the police.

When Robert and his brothers, sister and mother washed the family car when he was growing up, they always found ski masks and flashlights inside. Robert said a recent newspaper story also referred to the suspect's odor of gas or oil. This scared him because he claimed you could not help but get that smell on you after being in that flatbed tow truck. Robert's fiancée agreed.

I asked them if they could bring the truck to the police department, but Robert said it was parked at his grandfather's home in Canton and his grandfather would never allow him to do that.

In addition, Robert said his father had stopped to see him on May 21st, with a six-pack of beer. The son said his father left in a huff, in the grandfather's blue station wagon, after he drank two beers and got into an argument on the phone with Robert's mother, Marilyn. When I asked Robert what his father was wearing, Robert recalled a Michigan sweatshirt. Robert's fiancée also said that on another occasion when she helped Robert clean the truck they found ammunition and a gun clip under the front seat along with a ski mask. I took a taped statement from both of them.

After they left, I told Detective Machan about the interview with Griffith Sr. and my conviction that the father told his son whatever had been discussed with Detective Boerner and me. I felt that we were going to need a lot of luck to locate those tennis shoes.

..."*When I asked him if there were any truth to the allegations, he nodded yes*"...

Robert Griffith, Akron Beacon Journal, August 1988

Chapter 12

Detective Machan and I went to the Griffith home to serve the arrest warrants issued by the Massillon Municipal Court. We made regular trips there to see if we could catch him. Meanwhile, William Sr. was developing a great dislike for me. On one particular day, Maudie answered the door and showed us inside. We went to the living room area off the foyer and sat on a sofa. William Sr. was in a chair and Maudie sat by him.

I asked if their son was home and William Sr. snapped a "no" and added that if we wanted to search the house we could, but that the parents had no contact with Bill. I told William Sr. that it would not be necessary to search the house and that we would continue coming until we could locate his son.

At that point William Sr., who bore an uncanny resemblance to W.C. Fields, rose from his chair and roared, "God damn it, Ruby, I'm tired of this. I'm going to contact my attorney and put a lawsuit on your ass." Maudie then stood up and began to swoon, and dropped limp into her husband's arms. William was furious and yelled in an authoritative voice, "Heidi! Sick those sons-of-bitches." Machan and I looked at one another and could hear the faint sound of toe nails on linoleum. We quickly rose from our seats and bolted for the front door.

I'm a round kind of chubby guy and Mark Machan was shaped like a pear, except wider. We arrived at the door at the same time and got wedged there for a moment or two until we popped out onto the front porch. Simultaneously, the screen door slammed shut behind us as a large, black Doberman pinscher smashed into the screen door. The door bowed out to the breaking point and we drew our guns, thinking the dog was going to dine on us. Thankfully, the door held and we each remained in one piece.

From that day forward, whenever we stopped to see if William Jr. was there, Maudie would faint and her husband would curse me. It was like a routine that they had down pat. On occasion, William Sr. would be standing on the porch and I'd drive by and he would shake his fist and yell, "Ruby, God damn you." He reminded me of the Colonel Klink character on television's *Hogan's Heroes* show, who would shake his fist and mutter, "Hoooogann!"

I also had been talking on the phone with Marilyn Griffith for a few weeks to see if I could speak with her in person about her husband. She had been putting this off and was leery about talking to anyone. On June 17th she called and agreed to talk at her Hartville home. I contacted Swanson to go since he was familiar with most of the cases.

Marilyn was a pleasant woman, but it was obvious that the stress was wearing her down. She was concerned about strange occurrences around the house the past couple of weeks. She said that someone had pried a basement window open as well as the back door to the house. She said that her brother and parents had been experiencing hang-up phone calls and prowlers.

Swanson and I advised Marilyn about some precautions she could take and that she should call the sheriff or Uniontown police if she had any immediate needs. Marilyn said she felt Bill was behind all the harassment or it could be some of his friends from his car business. She provided the names of several people she thought could be involved. Eventually, the conversation came around to her husband.

Marilyn was visibly upset about everything that had happened over the previous two months. Newspaper stories, constant calls from the police, strangers, different media outlets, everyone wanting information. She was desperately trying to hold her family together and shield her children from the carnival atmosphere around them. It was very apparent to me that this woman and her children were victims, too.

Marilyn related how she had met Bill, the shooting in Akron, his job hopping the past two decades and his unusual nocturnal activity. She said she knew about his voyeurism problem, but that she could not bring herself to believe he was capable of committing rape. She said they had a normal sex life. As she put it, Bill was never violent with her or kinky.

Marilyn also said the marriage now was at a point of no return and that she was going to file for divorce. In a breaking voice, she explained her recent uneasiness with Bill pushing her to move to Oklahoma and uproot the family. She looked at Swanson and me and said that she had a gut feeling that Bill wanted to move her out there so he could kill her.

While they were married, Bill had at least two affairs that she knew about and possibly more. She added that he took care of the family financially, and the children did not lack for anything in that regard. She confirmed earlier stories from Robert, regarding the ski masks, flashlights and screwdrivers found in family vehicles over the years.

Marilyn said Bill would never admit that he had a voyeurism problem or undertake counseling unless he was arrested. She suggested that the police might want to talk to Dr. Brooks, Bill's former counselor.

I told her that I had recently spoken with people from

Emerge Ministries and that they said Bill had been in touch with them during the previous two weeks. He had asked their help for admission to a mental institution for his voyeurism problem because he was having a breakdown. I noted that the people from Emerge had declined to assist because Bill's criminal matters needed to be dealt with first.

Marilyn confirmed that Bill was home on April 12th when the Melissa Brown attack occurred and that on the evening of the 12th she had taken him to the airport for his return flight to Oklahoma.

Marilyn said Bill used the flatbed tow truck while he was in town that weekend, and that when she did the laundry on April 16th she found a strange pair of women's panties that did not belong to her or her daughter. She said she confronted Bill with her discovery and he told her they were probably his mother's and that she was overreacting. Marilyn said they had a huge argument, which culminated with her demand that he move out. She said Bill agreed and moved in with his parents and took some of his belongings with him.

Marilyn recalled an article in a March 1988 edition of the *Free Press (weekly Community Newspaper)* that referred to a string of unsolved rapes in Stark County over the last decade. The article gave her pause. She showed the article to her son Robert and they had talked about the possibility Bill could be involved. They thought it was possible and did not speak of it again until the recent deluge of publicity.

Before we left, I asked Marilyn if Bill had any belongings at the house or if he had taken everything to his parents' home. Marilyn said we were free to look through what Bill had left there. She led us to the family room where we saw a small mountain of clothing and shoes in a pile in the middle of the room. I noticed some of the shoes were TENNIS SHOES!

I went back to the dining room table to get my file that

included the photo-copy of the tennis shoe print Dennis Florea gave me more than a month before. I walked to the pile of clothing and picked up a pair of white tennis shoes and turned them over. I was almost too excited to form words. "Take a look at these," I said to Swanson. Tim looked at the shoes and the photocopy I had in my hand and said he thought they looked like a "match." I asked Marilyn if I could take the shoes and that I would give her a receipt. Marilyn said that the shoes had been sitting there since Bill moved out in April and that he had not come back to get the rest of his things. How lucky can you get? I thought. That would mean the wear pattern would *NOT* have changed!

Outside, I put the shoes in a bag in my trunk and told Swanson I was going straight to the crime lab to give the shoes to Florea. I broke every traffic law on my way. I radioed dispatch and asked them to call Florea to tell him what I thought I had. When I arrived, Bob Budgake and Florea took control of the shoes. Florea took a quick look and said they looked promising and that he would have to take his time and begin to do his analysis. I was ecstatic.

On June 21st, Florea called me and said that his analysis was complete and that Budgake corroborated his work. "These are positively the shoes from the Brown crime scene," Florea told me. Florea said that he would notify the county prosecutor about the developments after completing the paperwork. Recalling that phone conversation now, I could hardly believe the news. It meant we had Griffith! We could charge him with rape. The work that followed was like sipping water from a fire hose. It came fast and furious. We had to locate William Griffith Jr.!

*…"I am very much relieved"…"we have some victims
that have been terrified"…*

Robert Horowitz, former Stark County Prosecutor
Canton Repository, December 17, 1988

Chapter 13

On June 22, 1988, Tim Swanson and I met at the Jackson
Police Department and began to go over all the old rape case
files. We put together a spreadsheet identifying the police
agency case number, date, victim's name, crime location,
description of attacker and method of entry with a short
synopsis of each attack and what, if any, physical evidence
each scene yielded (*i.e.*, latent fingerprints, tool marks, rape
kits).

We did all this while also checking out a plethora of
tips that kept coming in regarding Bill Griffith's whereabouts.
The tips came in by the ton. Everyone saw him everywhere.
The irony was over the past 10 years, it was very true. Griffith
had been everywhere.

As the days and weeks passed, I prepared search-
warrant affidavits, obtained court orders and testified at
grand jury proceedings so that the grand jury could issue
subpoenas. I needed to obtain copies of credit card
statements, detailed copies of telephone bills that contained
numbers dialed and received, the placement of a mail cover at
the residence of William Griffith Sr. to keep track of his
incoming mail, and the placement of a pen register mechanical
device on the telephone line of William Griffith Sr. to keep
track of incoming and outgoing telephone numbers to and
from William Sr.'s residence.

Robert Griffith informed me that his grandmother, Maudie, had confided to him that she had been in regular contact with his father. We blanketed everything related to William and Maudie Griffith in an attempt to locate their son.

On July 7, William E. Griffith Jr. signed himself out of the Golden Valley Mental Health Center and, accompanied by his parents, drove to a Red Roof Inn in Grand Blanc, Michigan. His parents brought Bill's dog, Duke, a black German shepherd. Four days later, Griffith's parents put down a $150 deposit on an apartment for their son at The Country House Apartments in Grand Blanc, Michigan. No one else knew Bill's whereabouts.

Then it happened. I was looking at the list of physical evidence accumulated at rape scenes in the conference room Swanson and I had taken over. As I glanced at papers, Chief Paar came into the room with his morning coffee and asked me how things were coming along. I asked the chief if he thought anyone had ever taken Griffith's fingerprint card from his prior arrests for voyeurism and had those prints compared to the unknown latent prints associated with past rape cases? After a few moments of silence, Paar said, "Oh, they had to. Do you have any lab reports showing they had been compared either here or at BCI?" I responded, "Nope." We looked at each other in stunned silence. No one had taken the basic step of taking Griffith's fingerprint card to the crime lab to compare it to the unknown latent fingerprints to either identify him or eliminate him as the ski-mask rapist!

I told the chief I had to go to the Portage County Sheriff's Office to see a detective there about the Portage County rape cases and while there I would get a copy of Griffith's fingerprint card and take it to the BCI crime lab in Richfield, Ohio, for comparison. After BCI personnel had processed Jackson crime scenes, they retained the unidentified latent prints at their office. Since I was going to be in the area I would see if any prints could be identified from the early attacks. It was July 11th when I stopped at the BCI lab. The fingerprint examiner took the card containing Bill Griffith's inked fingerprint impressions.

The next day I received a call from the examiner. She had compared Griffith's fingerprints to the unidentified latent prints from the 1980 attack of Mary Westover. From his fingerprint card she had matched two fingers on Griffith's right hand and a partial palm print from his right palm to the unidentified latent prints in the Westover case. I could barely contain myself as I called Chief Paar and the Stark County prosecutor.

Later that day, I received arrest warrants from the Massillon City prosecutor's office. They charged William E Griffith Jr. with one count of rape and one count of aggravated burglary for the 1980 attack on Mary Westover and similar counts for the April 1988 attack on Melissa Brown.

The county prosecutor's office was in the process of preparing these cases for grand jury proceedings. Issuing warrants spanning the beginning to the end of these unsolved cases set off an additional firestorm of media attention. Bill Griffith's photograph appeared in nightly news broadcasts around Northeast Ohio and in every edition of area newspapers. Griffith had to be located.

On July 13th, Robert Griffith called to tell me that he had spoken with his grandmother and believed that his father was in a Golden Valley, Minnesota, mental health center. This information fit with phone numbers on the Ohio Bell phone bills that had been subpoenaed. I contacted the mental health center, but due to patient confidentiality, no one would say anything without a court order.

An approach was developed for locating Griffith. Jackson Township police immediately involved the FBI with its resources. William Downey, the FBI's agent in charge in Canton, obtained a federal warrant on July 14th, charging

Griffith with Unlawful Flight to Avoid Prosecution (UFAP), which enabled the FBI to obtain jurisdiction and join the hunt. At that point, based on interviews with Robert Griffith, the assumption was that Griffith was in Golden Valley.

On July 15th, Bill paid $200 in advance for his August rent. He also paid for his stay at the Red Roof Inn in Grand Blanc. And on the 16th, Griffith paid for a new sofa at the Naked City Furniture Store in Flint, Michigan, using his father's VISA card from Ameritrust Bank.

On July 18th, I received another call from Robert Griffith. He had learned from his grandmother, Maudie that his father had spoken to her twice in the last three days.

I obtained a search warrant to secure hair samples from Griffith Jr.'s German shepherd, Duke. Oddly enough the search warrant was signed by then Stark County Common Pleas Court Judge James Unger, who had been Stark County Prosecutor when Griffith's spree started in 1980.

Earlier, Stark County Crime Lab Criminalist Michelle Mitchell had determined that some unknown hairs located at the scene of the Melissa Brown attack were animal hairs and, most probably, dog hairs. Marilyn and Robert Griffith had said that Bill had taken his dog to his parents' home. I arrived at the home of the elder Griffiths at 9:40 a.m. with Detective Machan, Stark County Animal Control Officers, two Canton police officers, Michelle Mitchell and a Canton fire rescue squad.

I knocked on the back door. When Maudie saw the small army of officers, she promptly fainted. This was the reason for bringing the rescue squad. Authorities stepped over the fallen Maudie and entered the residence in search of Duke. Medics got Maudie onto the living room couch. Animal control officers looked in the basement, the second level of the home, and in the attic. I followed along as William Sr. followed me at my heels and breathed down my neck. He was furious.

There was no sign of Duke. As the medics prepared to take Maudie to the hospital, she begged uniformed officers for a gun so she could "end it all." William Griffith Sr. threatened me with another lawsuit as I informed him his son was now wanted for rape along with the voyeurism charges.

Detective Machan and I, along with Michelle Mitchell, then went to a Prospect Street address in Hartville. Marilyn was living there now and we had to serve a search warrant for hair samples from Sounder, a yellow Labrador retriever, who still lived with her. Mitchell was able to collect the samples.

Tom Kell of the Stark County prosecutor's office called that afternoon and told me a package of information from the Golden Valley Mental Health Center had arrived. In reading the material, I learned Griffith had left the center on July 7th. No one there knew where he might be headed. I called the facility's administrator, who said that when he left the facility Griffith had been prescribed medication and was instructed to call when he needed a refill. The facility would notify the pharmacy where he wanted the prescription refilled that it would be okay to do it. The administrator assured me he would let me know where the pharmacy was located if Griffith called.

The Golden Valley administrator called me on July 30th, to report that Griffith had phoned him when he was out and left a message to return the call. The phone number was for a Red Roof Inn in Flint, Michigan. I promptly called Flint Police Lt. Jerry Dickensen, who was in charge of their fugitive unit. Dickensen asked me to forward my request through NCIC and said he would assemble a team to check it out right away. A little over an hour later, Dickensen said Griffith was no longer there. He said that Griffith had checked in on July 10th and checked out seven days later.

Following a host of unsuccessful leads, I had to admit that we had no idea where William E Griffith Jr. was. We had just missed him in Golden Valley, Minnesota, and Flint and

Grand Blanc, Michigan.

On August 8th and 9th, Kell advised me about a large amount of information Ohio Bell had sent in response to our subpoenas. What I learned made me laugh. I discovered what Griffith Sr. had been up to.

He had a calling card from Ohio Bell. We were aware from friends and relatives that William Sr. was suspicious of all law enforcement personnel. He thought he was being watched and thought his phone was being tapped, so he would leave his residence and go to an outside phone booth at a convenience store on Woodland Avenue at 15th Street N.W. in Canton. Based on his calling card instructions, he would dial his home number before dialing the number he wanted to call.

After reviewing the subpoenaed information, I discovered a delay in obtaining the information because of William Sr.'s antics. However, since Ohio Bell account information had been subpoenaed in conjunction with his billing and toll records, we were able to see where he called. I looked at all the June and July calls to Golden Valley and Grand Blanc. The entire time that he and his wife maintained they had no idea where their son was or what he was doing, they had been helping their son elude authorities.

On August 12th at 9 p.m., a Jackson police dispatcher notified me at home about a phone call from a gentleman at Golden Valley who wanted to talk to me right away. The man told the dispatcher it was an emergency. I called the number and a man named *Mark Frazier* answered. He introduced himself as William Griffith Jr.'s case manager at Golden Valley Mental Health Center.

Frazier said that he had received a telephone call about an hour earlier from a man named *Tim Tesh*, who had been Bill Griffith's Golden Valley roommate. Tesh informed Frazier that, at his invitation, Griffith had moved to Phoenix,

Arizona. Since his arrival, according to Tesh, Griffith seemed to be regressing with his sexual issues.

Tesh told Frazier that he caught Bill stalking Tesh's sister and that Griffith tried to get in the back door of her home. My heart was pumping wildly when Frazier said the counselor had already phoned Phoenix police to let them know that Griffith was wanted in Ohio for multiple rapes. Frazier said he also advised Tesh that Griffith was dangerous. Frazier gave me Tesh's phone number. The Jackson police dispatcher supplied the number for the Phoenix police and then sent them a teletype via NCIC to contact Jackson ASAP (as soon as possible) in reference to William E Griffith Jr.

My mind was racing as I dialed Tesh's number. I could envision losing Griffith again after being so close. Tesh said that he had called Tucson police to watch his house in case Griffith arrived. He said he was shocked to hear about Griffith's issues in Ohio, but he said he always thought Griffith was hiding something about himself. I got Tesh's assurance that he would not call or tip off his friend, but I needed desperately to call the Phoenix police to alert them about Griffith before anyone went out looking for him.

Within a few minutes I spoke with Phoenix Police Detective Dave Swearingen, who affirmed receipt of the teletype and his earlier phone call from the Minnesota clinic about Griffith and his arrest warrants. Swearingen advised me that he was assembling a team of undercover officers for backup before he and his partner went out to Apartment 136 on East Thomas Street in Phoenix.

After I got off the phone with Swearingen, I called Swanson to bring him up to speed on developments. I told him that I did not have a phone number to contact FBI Special Agent Larry Setmeyer. Swanson said he knew how to contact him and would let the FBI know Griffith was in Phoenix.

At approximately midnight on August 12th, Detective

Swearingen called and told me that he was sitting at his desk and across from him was William E. Griffith Jr. in handcuffs!

I was blown away. We finally had him. Swearingen told me that he and his partner had gone to Griffith's apartment complex and located his red Mercury Lynx in the parking lot. They were watching it, while waiting for additional units to arrive, when Griffith got into the vehicle. He said they followed him for a little more than two miles as they radioed for backup from marked patrol units. Swearingen said Griffith pulled into the parking lot of the Sunburst Resort Hotel and parked his car. He was then quickly approached and taken into custody without incident.

Swearingen asked me if there was anything further I wanted him to do. I asked if they had any plans to interview Griffith. He said that they were about to do that, but he wanted to let me know they had apprehended Griffith. I asked Swearingen if he could get a search warrant for Griffith's apartment and that I wanted him to look for any handwritten journals that Griffith may have kept that detailed his sexual fantasies or his acts of sexual violence. Swearingen told me that he would take care of the requests over the next several hours. He said Griffith already informed him that he would consent to a search of his apartment.

"Now that the police have caught him and this charge has been dropped, it's like pouring salt in my wounds...he's never going to feel the anger and the disgust and the fears I have"...

1980 rape victim from Jackson Township whose case was outside the statute of limitations and was dismissed despite Griffith's fingerprints found at the scene
Akron Beacon Journal, September 4, 1988

Chapter 14

On Monday, August 15th, 1988, Jackson Township Police Chief Philip Paar, Stark County Sheriff's Detective Tim Swanson, Investigator Tom Kell from the Stark County Prosecutor's Office, and I met with Assistant Stark County Prosecutor Paul Mastriacovo and Chief Counsel Richard Reinbold about the events three nights earlier that led to Griffith's capture.

The prosecutors wanted to know if Griffith would waive extradition from Arizona. They began figuring when time officially began ticking as it related to a potential criminal trial. Normally, if a felony defendant was being held, he had 90 days before the trial had to begin.

Then William Downey, the FBI's supervising agent in Canton, telephoned Swanson to request that those in the meeting come to his office to debrief him about the capture of Griffith. Downey was upset about the exchange of information on that previous Friday night and how Phoenix police and the FBI sought Griffith in an uncoordinated effort, which he thought potentially, could have resulted in someone getting hurt.

Prior to this meeting, I had never met Downey. I could tell instantly Downey was a taskmaster and did not stand for any nonsense. At first, I was taken aback by Downey's scolding of Chief Paar and Swanson. Downey did not even know I was in the room until Tim Swanson said, "Bill, this can all be explained, if you'd let this guy talk." Swanson pointed at me.

I introduced myself and explained that I did not have any way of contacting Special Agent Setmeyer on Friday night and that I was not about to lose another opportunity to capture Griffith when we were so close. Downey informed me about proper protocol for cases in the future.

It was decided that Swanson and I would fly out later that day to Phoenix to escort Bill Griffith back to Canton, Ohio. Prior to the flight out of Cleveland Hopkins Airport, authorities in Phoenix said that Griffith had waived any extradition proceedings and could be picked up anytime. Griffith, however, told officials in Phoenix that he would not return to Ohio if they sent "that asshole Detective Rudy. He's ruined my life by spreading malicious rumors about me," he told Arizona authorities.

The lieutenant in charge of the proceedings in Phoenix said, "You may want to reconsider sending this Detective Rudy out here because Griffith gets real agitated when he starts discussing him." Well, I can tell you there was no way in hell I was going to be kept from that trip. I decided to tell them I was Jackson Township Detective Mark Machan (with whom I worked).

Swanson and I arrived in Phoenix on the evening of August 15th. We went to our hotel and then called Phoenix police. We said that we wanted to see Griffith and possibly interview him, if Griffith wanted to talk. Phoenix police sent a detective to pick us up and then took us to one of the eight jail sites that made up the Maricopa County jail system. At that time they had eight different locations and 8,000 inmates in their county jail! We ended up visiting three different locations until we found the one where William Griffith was housed. We were shown to an interview room and told Griffith would meet us and that we could use the room as long as we needed.

After a short wait, a corrections officer came in with William E. Griffith Jr. He wore orange coveralls and was not handcuffed. Swanson introduced himself to Griffith and then Griffith put out his hand to me. Before I could say, "Hi, I'm Mark Machan," Griffith said, "You're Chris Rudy, aren't you?" I said, "No, I'm Mark Machan." The hair stood up on the back of my neck. We spoke to him for a short time and Griffith never took his eyes off me. He indicated that he had an attorney and would not answer questions without his attorney present. Three times Griffith asked if I was Chris Rudy and I insisted I was Mark Machan. Griffith was taken back to his cell and arrangements were made to pick him up the next morning with an escort to the airport for the flight back to Canton.

When Swanson and I got back to the hotel, Swanson broke out in uproarious laughter. "You should have seen the look on your face when he said, 'You're Chris Rudy, aren't you.' You looked like you were pissing your pants," Swanson said. I have to admit I was pretty shocked as Griffith never took his eyes off me and with Griffith's insistence that I was Chris Rudy.

The next morning we picked up Griffith, boarded the plane, and headed to Chicago for a connecting flight. When we were seated and preparing for take-off, Griffith, who was seated between us, leaned over to me and said, "You're Chris Rudy, aren't you?" "No, I'm Mark. I told you that," I insisted. I could see Swanson was smiling and shaking his head.

When the flight landed at O'Hare Airport, we were the last people to get off the plane. We were surprised to discover that someone had asked the Chicago PD to stand by until the flight to Canton was ready to depart. With two uniformed officers we started to walk through the terminal. Griffith wore a suit and had his sport coat draped over his handcuffs in front of him. The shorter of the two officers touched my arm to let Swanson and the other officer walk ahead with Griffith so he could talk to me.

The officer asked me what was so important about Griffith that we needed babysitting. "What'd this guy do?" he asked. I told him Griffith faced several charges of rape, but figured him for many, many more. The officer asked, "Have you interviewed him yet?" When I said we would wait until we got back to Canton, he offered a room. "Well, if you want, the airline lets us use some office space here for our interviews. We can let you guys use it for awhile so you can slap him around for awhile to get him ready for your interview."

"Na," I said. "Thanks for the offer, but I don't want to show up with all the media there and him looking like that." The Chicago officer replied, "Okay, it's your choice."

Several hours later we were back in Canton and took Griffith to the Jackson Township Police Department, where he was photographed and fingerprinted. Swanson went home and I had Griffith in my detective bureau office. At that time I extended my hand to Griffith and told him, "Yes, I'm Chris Rudy." Griffith responded, "I knew you were." I told him we were told he would fight extradition if I came out to Phoenix, so that was why I kept telling Griffith I was Mark Machan.

I had about 20 minutes with Griffith before I had him taken to the Massillon city jail. I laid out everything for Griffith I knew about him. His fingerprints were found at past scenes and he was going to be the first DNA case in Stark County. I promised Griffith that police would tie all the cases together and that he would never be free.

Griffith told me that he would love to talk and clear up everything, but he wanted to meet first with his attorney. I told Griffith that he had every right to do that, and went on to explain that I was not trying to get him to break down to get him to start to talk. I wanted to tell him exactly what was about to happen to him. I told him I wanted the opportunity to be the first to let him know what was coming. If he chose to remain silent that was fine, because we had him whether he wanted to talk or not.

Two uniformed officers transported Griffith to the jail and booked him. I have never spoken to William Griffith Jr. since that day, though I have tried numerous times since, but Griffith always refused.

Over the next few days I spoke with Detective Dave Swearingen in Phoenix. Swearingen told me that Griffith had worked about two weeks for a Dodge dealership in Scottsdale, Arizona, before his arrest. His search of Griffith's apartment had yielded 19 brown spiral notebooks, which contained sexual information from Griffith's hospital stay, a red folder with notes about women he had been with, numerous letters he had written to women he had contacted through a "singles" newspaper, a personal journal, a booklet on women and sexual addiction, and the "Sexual Inventory of Bill Griffith." I asked Swearingen to send these items at his earliest convenience along with Griffith's signed consent form.

Detective Swearingen also said that he had interviewed Tim Tesh and his younger sister, *Alice,* who had gone out with Griffith. He said that Alice was very afraid of Griffith after he looked in her bedroom window after a date. Her mother and a neighbor saw him and yelled at him, which caused him to run away. Alice said she refused to speak to him afterward. However, the next day, he followed her when she went to and from work.

Swearingen said that her brother, Tim, told him about the first time Bill went out with his sister. Bill came by the house the next day while his sister was at work and asked Tim's brother if he could go into Alice's bedroom and put a red rose on her bed. Tim's brother would not allow it and Bill left disappointed.

According to the detective, when his brother told Tim about the encounter Tim knew what Bill was up to. He said Bill admitted in group therapy at Golden Valley that he had a "panty fetish" and liked to take women's underwear with which he masturbated. Tim claimed that Bill was trying to get a pair of his sister's panties. I asked Swearingen to forward a report about these incidents. Swearingen said he would do so as soon as possible.

On August 22nd, the Stark County grand jury indicted William Griffith Jr. for rape and aggravated burglary in the April 12, 1988, attack on Melissa Brown. The voyeurism charges for the Daytona and Hills & Dales Street incidents were dismissed. Also, the statute of limitations had expired on the 1980 rape charge of Mary Westover, so the warrant charging Griffith with her rape was dismissed. It was unbelievable to everyone involved that all arguments about the inapplicability of the statute of limitations had failed. This information also set off a firestorm of protests from the community and area legislators to change the statute of limitations in rape cases and other felony charges. Stark County Common Pleas Court Judge James Unger ordered Griffith to surrender blood, hair and saliva samples for DNA testing purposes. Unger had come full circle with the Stark County ski-mask rapist. He started out six years earlier as the county prosecutor putting together a task force and now was a county judge ordering tests after the defendant's arrest.

Three days later, the fingerprints of William Griffith Jr. were positively matched to latent prints lifted from the Debbie Waltz crime scene. She was raped in her home in July 1980. This crime too was outside the statute of limitations, so Griffith could not be charged. Part way through this investigation I had been surprised that no one had thought to take the elementary step of comparing Griffith's fingerprint card against latent prints from earlier attacks. During the time leading up to Griffith's trial date, I asked Tim Swanson why no one had ever done that. I thought all these cases likely would have been solved years earlier. Swanson explained that when you work on a large-scale case like the Griffith investigation you can develop tunnel vision and miss the simple things. He said that it was important to have a set of fresh eyes take a look at the case. Often simple things would jump out.

For a couple of weeks after Griffith returned from Arizona, I kept after prosecutors to indict his parents, Maudie and William Sr. I was outraged over their behind-the-scenes machinations and felt that charges were appropriate. Charges never were filed against the parents. A prosecutor told me they were focused on the big prize. They had the rapist and wanted a conviction. His parents did what any parent would do for their child under the circumstances. I never agreed with that rationale. However, how often do detectives and prosecutors agree on charges?

On August 30th and 31st, reports from the Stark County Crime Lab were made public. They confirmed positive matches in blood typing work between Melissa Brown's rape kit and samples taken from William Griffith Jr. The Crime Lab, in consultation with the Stark County prosecutor's office, then decided on a DNA testing facility. Samples from Melissa Brown and past victims would be sent for testing purposes to Forensic Science Associates in Richmond, California, near San Francisco. By 1988 standards the cost of the test was exorbitant. The test for Brown's case alone would be $5,000. This was historic for Stark County as it was the first time DNA evidence would be used locally. On August 13th, 1988, Montgomery County prosecutors in Dayton, Ohio, successfully convicted Gary R. Dascenzo of the kidnapping and murder of a Columbus, Ohio, woman. Until then, the use of DNA evidence had yet to be tested in Ohio courts.

In September, Tom Kell was busy contacting former victims of Griffith. He used the chart that Swanson and I made. The victims met Kell at the Canton Health Department in order to provide saliva and blood samples to send to the California lab chosen for DNA testing. In all, 18 Stark County women were willing to provide samples. The total cost of the testing was expected to exceed $100,000. On September 18th, the samples of Melissa Brown and William E. Griffith Jr. were sent to California to be tested. Griffith's trial was scheduled for the middle of October. However, the DNA testing would delay the trial until December.

As the trial date drew near, defense attorney James Burdon of Akron and Assistant Stark Prosecutor Paul Mastriacovo argued behind the scenes until a plea agreement was reached. Attorneys on both sides were advised DNA testing would not be complete until February 1989, which caused yet another delay. In the meantime, news media across the region speculated that Griffith was responsible for 50, 60 or 70 rapes over the past decade.

On December 15th, William E. Griffith Jr. pled guilty to one count each of rape and aggravated burglary for the attack on Melissa Brown eight months earlier. Stark Common Pleas Court Judge Sheila Farmer gave Griffith the maximum sentence of 10 to 25 years on each count, to be served consecutively, for an actual sentence of 20 to 50 years of incarceration.

When Griffith agreed to plead guilty, the prosecutor's office cancelled additional testing due to the high cost of DNA testing.

Prior to Griffith's plea, Stark County Prosecutor Robert Horowitz took Chief Paar, Mastriacovo and me to lunch at Bender's Tavern in downtown Canton. Horowitz congratulated all involved for their efforts in the case and said, "William Griffith is the most dangerous man I believe I've ever put away to this day." That statement has stayed with me and I have no doubt that it was very true.

Mastriacovo was the lead prosecutor against Griffith.

He had been an assistant county prosecutor for 20 years. When I asked what his feelings were prosecuting a man like Griffith, knowing what Griffith had done to his victims, families, and neighborhoods, Mastriacovo's response was typical – exactly what you would expect.

He said that he never let his personal feelings or emotions get in the way of professional decisions. Mastriacovo recalled the work and research that he undertook as this was the first DNA case in Stark County. He had to research the scientific aspects of DNA and the admissibility of this new type of scientific evidence in a criminal case in Ohio. Mastriacovo addressed the question of technology (DNA and AFIS) and its use in identifying and capturing serial rapists. He felt that every legitimate, ethical, and legal law enforcement tool is valuable. He pointed out that sometimes (even when there is a test linking a suspect to a crime) the victim does not cooperate, which frustrates both law enforcement and prosecutors. Sometimes there is a very strong case prior to forensic analysis that an inconclusive test result weakens. Each case is unique. Mastriacovo added that most people, and he included himself, were appalled at the series of rape cases during the 1980's.

Paula Smith was the Director of the Rape Crisis Center in Stark County from 1982 to 1985 and went directly from there to a new position as coordinator of the prosecutor's Victim Assistance program. That job evolved into her current position as director of the prosecutor's Victim/Witness Division. Mrs. Smith recalled that while at the Rape Crisis Center numerous callers described a man wearing a ski mask, who cut a window screen, broke a window and succeeded in sexually assaulting them. She said that it did not take long for her and other call-takers to believe these reports were linked to one person. She said the staff had to be careful, due to confidentiality issues, as to what they said to law enforcement personnel. She said the callers often crossed jurisdictional lines, so she would tell one department or another, "You may want to talk to this police department because they had something similar occur in their jurisdiction recently. Law enforcement was great to work with, they were anxious to apprehend the person committing these crimes," she said.

"There was such a long period of time during (which) these rapes occurred, and everyone hoped the person would be caught. My group from Rape Crisis was deluged with information requests for Neighborhood Crime Watch meetings. People living in apartments became upset with landlords if they didn't install security measures, such as operable locks on windows and deadbolt key locks on doors. People wanted to feel safe in their homes. We also had numerous requests for self-defense classes, too."

Paula Smith added, "The first two detectives I worked with on the rapes were Dino Borello and Tim Swanson from the Stark County Sheriff's Department. They had so many attacks in their jurisdiction. Then Detective Chris Rudy from Jackson Township joined them. They worked tirelessly trying to solve these cases. These three men, in particular, were kind and sensitive to the victims and thorough in their investigations. They put in extremely long hours, and I doubt that the community ever really knew of the time and effort that these men and law enforcement in general put forth in matters such as these.

"I recall the relief felt in the community when William Griffith was caught in Arizona. However, I was concerned about the next phase for all the victims. They would have to face the accused and relive the nightmare in open court." She knew it would surely open many old wounds.

"All these victims had been traumatized by what they experienced, and it had taken a long time for their individual healing processes to begin. So when they heard the news they called in asking, 'Will I have to go to court? Will I have to testify? I don't want to see him!'"

Another primary player in the Griffith case was Judge Sheila Farmer, a veteran Stark County jurist and the presiding judge in the Griffith trial. The judge recalled that the six-year statute of limitations controlled what the prosecutor planned to do. She explained that usually the prosecutor picks the best cases and takes those to trial. DNA, she noted, was brand new 23 years ago, though now it is used to get people out of prison as well as to put them inside.

The judge noted that a pre-sentence investigation was not done in the Griffith case because of the plea bargain struck by the prosecutor's office and Griffith's attorney. She said that Griffith just stood there at sentencing. "He didn't speak, and I didn't expect him to." The judge explained that "the reason for the plea deal is that you don't want to traumatize these people [victims] anymore than they already are, if you have accomplished a long enough sentence. In this instance, I couldn't have added anymore [time] to it. Everyone agreed it was the best deal that could be had. I think he (Griffith) is a noteworthy criminal for this area. We don't have a lot of serial rapists in Stark County. We don't have a lot of serial criminals for that matter."

*"I've never had a problem with drugs.
I've had a problem with the police."*

*Keith Richards, English musician, songwriter and
founding member of The Rolling Stones*

Chapter 15

In the summer of 1992, Portage County Sheriff's Detective Cindy Balog called me to ask whatever happened in the William E. Griffith Jr. case.

Balog told me that she was assigned to clean the property room at the sheriff's office. While going through evidence related to the rape of Janet Higgins in February 1988, she found a rape kit that had samples which could be tested. She said the last supplements added to the Higgins case file suggested William Griffith was a strong suspect. The final supplement also noted Griffith's trial in Stark County, but no final outcome was listed. I told her what sentence Griffith had received and that he was incarcerated at the Lebanon Correctional Facility in Warren County, Ohio.

I told Detective Balog I believed it was worthwhile to have the samples tested since time still remained under the six-year statute of limitations. She also might determine if Griffith would consent to an interview. She proceeded with her follow-up investigation (along with her county prosecutor, David Norris), and decided to contact Griffith at Lebanon.

In a prison interview room, Bill Griffith told Balog he did not want to talk and he did not want to voluntarily contribute a DNA sample. In 1993, Griffith was moved to the Marion Correctional Institution. Balog obtained fresh samples of blood and saliva from Janet Higgins and then worked through the Portage County prosecutor and prison and court officials in Marion County to compel Griffith to furnish saliva and bodily fluids.

After Balog secured samples from both parties, Portage County officials sent the samples to the FBI lab in Washington, D.C., which had just recently started a DNA testing lab. After months of waiting, results showed that the man who attacked Janet Higgins was positively identified as William E. Griffith Jr.

Portage County indicted Griffith on one count of aggravated burglary and one count of rape. In the fall of 1994, during a hearing in Common Pleas Court, Bill Griffith pled guilty to the charges. In exchange, he received a sentence of "concurrent time," or no additional time to his current sentence. Also, as part of the agreement, Griffith had to sit down with Detective Balog and clear up any other rapes he committed in Portage County.

Balog had Griffith removed from his cell and brought to her office in the detective bureau. She arranged for a polygraph examiner as well. Balog told Griffith she wanted him to tell her about all the other rapes he had committed in Portage County. She also said she had a polygraph examiner there to satisfy her of Griffith's honesty.

Griffith told Balog he did not want to talk to her and that his attorney never informed him that he had to talk to her or any other official about anything else he may have done. Balog was incredulous. She told Griffith he had just signed a plea agreement earlier that day and that this interview was part of that agreement. Griffith assured her he was not trying to be difficult, but he declined to talk.

Balog called the Portage County prosecutor and informed him of what she was up against. He told her that he would talk to Griffith's attorney the next morning and tell him that his client was reneging on his part of the deal. Prosecutor Norris also told her to inform Griffith that, if needed, he would be indicted on further test results, his earlier guilty plea would be nullified and he would be tried for the Janet Higgins rape.

Balog informed Griffith of Norris' comments and had Griffith returned to his cell. The next afternoon Griffith was brought back to the detective bureau to tell Balog about the other crimes he had committed in Portage County. Also present was the polygraph examiner. Earlier Griffith had been visited by his attorney, who informed him that he had an obligation to disclose everything in reference to his past criminal activity in Portage County.

The detective spent more than eight hours with Griffith that day. She noted in her report that Griffith was not forthcoming. He was put on the polygraph machine twice and on both occasions was regarded as being untruthful. Griffith admitted that he had broken into two other homes in Portage County and raped two other women. Citing a faulty memory, he gave vague descriptions of the locations and attacks. Detective Balog was disgusted with Griffith. She said it was like pulling teeth to get him to candidly discuss what he had done.

She wrote in a report that Griffith should never be considered for parole and that, after spending six years in prison, he never showed the smallest glimmer of remorse for what he had done. Griffith blamed his compulsion for voyeurism for the rapes he committed. He said his victims just happened to be there, and his voyeuristic tendencies took over. Griffith claimed he never wanted to rape anyone. Balog had pressed Griffith to open up and help all his victims, not only those in Portage County but those in Stark County as well, achieve some sense of closure so they could move on with their lives. Balog noted that Griffith never denied there were other victims in Stark County or in other areas. He told her he only was willing to discuss the Portage County cases.

In the fall of 1992 William Griffith not only was dealing

with Portage County officials about his past crimes but also preparing to marry for the third time. I interviewed *Susan Marsh* while gathering background information on Griffith. The following information was provided by Susan about her relationship with William Griffith.

William E. Griffith Jr. had an affair with Susan Marsh while married to Marilyn. Susan was seven years younger than Griffith and was raised in the Summit County area of Northeast Ohio. When Bill entered her life she recalled that she was 20 and had a job at a restaurant at Summit Mall. One of her girlfriends, who worked at a clothing store in the mall, introduced her to Griffith during one of his visits to the store. Susan and Bill hit it off immediately. Susan dated Bill for several months. He helped her father, who worked as an insurance salesman. Her father became a top salesman with Bill's help. Her family just loved Bill, she said. She did not see him for a few weeks at a time, but did not think anything of it because Bill was also in sales and traveled a lot.

Susan recalled that Bill and his father had an apartment in Akron at that time. She and Bill had dated for several months, when her girlfriend from the clothing store told her that Bill had just been in the store and bought three women's coats. Bill told Susan's friend that "one is for Susan, one is for my sister and one is for my wife." The friend said Bill did not bat an eye, but Susan was dumbfounded as she never had any inkling that he was married.

She confronted Griffith with this information and he admitted he was married. Susan was upset because she had fallen in love with Bill. He said all the right things and was a wonderful person. After having met Bill's father, mother and sister, she could not believe that no one had told her that he was married. Yet they all knew he was cheating on his wife! Susan ended the relationship immediately.

Over the years, Susan married and had children of her own. In 1988, she received a phone call from Bill's sister whom she had befriended back when she was 20. Griffith's sister asked her if she would like to see Bill. Susan was 39 at the time and had been divorced for awhile. She said yes because she remembered Bill as a great guy.

They only saw each other for a few days. Bill admitted that he was still married to Marilyn, but they were separated. He told her about his first daughter, whom he had never met, and told Susan that he had four children with Marilyn. After briefly getting reacquainted, Bill was on the run. She read in the newspapers that he was accused of rape. His parents told her that he was being railroaded. She said she could not believe he was guilty because of the Bill Griffith she knew.

Over the next four years, Susan kept in close contact with Bill, his parents, his kids and some of his other family members. She visited them at their homes and hosted a baby shower for Bill's daughter.

Bill's mother told her how they would never lie to her again. Maudie confided that when Bill was released from Golden Valley Health Center in Minnesota they went to a lake or a river near a park somewhere in Michigan. Bill and his parents "wiped the slate clean" by throwing rocks into the water and promised to be honest with each other from there on out. Looking back, Susan said none of them were ever honest with her about anything; not about the rapes Bill had committed or about themselves.

During a solo visit with Bill while he was in prison, Bill admitted that he was a voyeur. "Now I want you to be honest with me about all this stuff," Susan told Bill. He told her that voyeurs do not rape and, therefore, he never raped anyone.

In the late fall of 1992, Susan agreed to marry Bill while he was incarcerated at the Lebanon Correctional Institution. By marrying him, Susan felt she was helping Bill get a chance at an early release from prison. She recalled that Bill's parents constantly encouraged her and told her that he would have a better chance at parole if he was married.

More than once Susan had mentioned meeting with Detective Rudy about Bill's case and his parents always discouraged her. They told her "how it would look bad for Bill" if she did that. Susan loved Bill, and his parents convinced her that the police had railroaded him and that he would get out of prison soon.

Early in 1993, Bill's first wife, Teresa Martin, told Bill's daughter, Doris, that her biological father was William Griffith. Like any adopted child, Doris wanted to meet her parent face to face. She contacted Bill's parents and went to Canton to meet everyone. Susan recalled that she and Doris hit it off right away. They planned a visit to Lebanon Correctional for that April. When they arrived, they met with Bill in the prison's cafeteria area. Along with Susan, Doris brought her husband and one of her sons, an infant at the time. They visited for about an hour and had lunch together.

After lunch, Bill suggested that it was not fair for Doris's husband and the baby to stay longer and suggested they return to the hotel. Since this was the first time he had ever seen Doris, he also asked Susan to sit at a separate table so he could have a private meeting with Doris. That afternoon was an eye-opening experience for Susan. She now maintains that she never before had seen this Bill Griffith. She remembered that he was kind of "glazed over" that afternoon. While she wanted to be understanding, because this was the first time Bill had met his daughter, she felt something was wrong. Something did not feel right.

According to Susan, Bill acted nervously all afternoon and got up and walked around. About 10 times he was escorted out to use the restroom and did not act himself. When she left with Doris she was shaking. She made up her mind then that as soon as she could she was going to contact me. She wanted to look at Bill's investigative file.

Susan and her sister later met with me. They looked at the case file and listened to my story of the investigation. When Susan left, she contacted an attorney that same day and started divorce proceedings against Bill. She had been married to Bill for approximately six months by the time the uncontested annulment was granted on February 7, 1994.

After she started divorce proceedings, Susan never heard from Bill's family. At one point, Bill sent her a typewriter. He wanted to continue correspondence, but she never replied. Susan felt betrayed by Bill's parents yet again. She said she should have acted on her gut feelings and contacted me months before, but she listened to his parents go on and on about how things that were not true were easily printed in the paper and that I did not have any proof Bill did anything.

I asked Susan what her relationship with Bill's parents was the second time she met them since they had lied to her before. Susan said she got along fine with Bill's dad, but she noticed he had quite a temper although he was always a perfect gentleman with her. Her interaction with Bill's mother was different. She was told that Maudie and one of her sisters had allegedly done something to Bill when he was a child. Susan said she believes that this was one of the things about which Bill and his parents had "wiped the slate clean" when they threw rocks in the water. She felt that whatever it was that happened to Bill as a child contributed to how he turned out as an adult.

I asked Susan how her family reacted in 1992 when she married someone in prison. She said they were not happy, but they gave her the benefit of the doubt since she had known Bill 20 years earlier. She also said her dad always liked Bill. Her family members had always said love is blind. "Boy, were they right," she told me. Susan added that she never had her name changed when she married Bill because she did not want anyone to know she was married to someone in prison.

Susan now believes William E. Griffith Jr. is guilty. She reflected on the question of how a man could be so loving to three wives and at the same time be so evil with all the women he harmed. She feels fortunate that she knew the kind and gentle Bill rather than the rapist. She also apologized to me. She had blocked out so much from her past with the Griffith family because it was such a bad part of her life. She reiterated how fortunate she felt now. The worst that happened to her was being lied to, and embarrassed about her foolish decisions.

She also expressed the hope that Griffith would eventually talk to me and admit all that he had done. She thought that this might be easier for him now that both his parents had died. She felt it would be a giant relief to him to get it all out and might possibly help someone reading this book realize one should get help instead of hurting other people.

Teresa Martin, Doris's mother, told me her daughter's life had been turned upside down after meeting her biological father. Doris spent her own money to pay attorney fees in an attempt to win her father's release from prison. In the end, it cost Doris her marriage. Bill manipulated Doris in the same way he manipulated his other children. Bill encouraged a belief amongst his children that he was innocent and would soon win his freedom.

In November 2003, Doris penned a letter to Melissa Brown, to ask her not to stand in the way of her father's attempt for parole. The letter was sent to Melissa at her residence accompanied by correspondence from the attorney whom Doris had hired for her father in February 2004.

Needless to say, the letter sent Melissa into panic. She contacted me mortified that her attacker's daughter was able to locate her. She was also aghast at the nerve of Doris and her attorney to ask her to stand down while Bill Griffith attempted to gain parole.

I read the letter. The contents revealed Doris had been manipulated by her father's lies of contriteness and rehabilitation. She believed her father would do well on the outside by counseling sex offenders, thereby changing their lives and reducing the number of future victims.

In my estimation, Griffith's children have been continuously victimized by their father through his constant manipulative ways.

"Force is all-conquering, but its victories are short-lived."

Abraham Lincoln, 1809-1865
16th President of the United States

Chapter 16

In 2002, the Ohio Bureau of Criminal Investigation had fully implemented the Combined DNA Index System (CODIS). The system provides a DNA data base of known offenders. Samples of known DNA can be matched against unknown DNA samples in order to identify the contributor of the unknown sample, much like the fingerprint identification system discussed earlier in this book. In 2002, the Ohio attorney general had requested police agencies around the state to submit unknown DNA samples to BCI in order to identify offenders linked to cold cases.

In October 2003, officials from the Miami County prosecutor's office and the Miami County Sheriff's Office met to discuss positive DNA test results they had received from BCI. Prosecutors in Miami County concluded that the identification of William E. Griffith Jr. as the unknown contributor of sample DNA from rapes committed in 1986 presented a prosecution problem since the statute of limitations at the time of the attacks was six years. Fifteen years after his incarceration for the attack on Melissa Brown, Bill Griffith was again identified from evidence collected in the long string of attacks during the 1980's. It was not until August 2005 that Miami County sheriff's investigators visited Griffith at the Richland Correctional Institution to ask him why his DNA was found at the scene of those 1986 incidents.

At their initial meeting, Griffith refused to speak, citing advice from his attorney. Miami County detectives then discovered that Griffith's attorney had been disbarred so they attempted to speak with Griffith again. However, this time they informed Griffith that he was not going to be prosecuted because of the statute of limitations.

On September 15, 2005, Bill Griffith agreed to be interviewed by Miami County investigators, but he would not write anything nor would he consent to be recorded. The investigators agreed and Griffith admitted that he had been in the area at the relevant time. He said he had business in the area and was driving his car hauler for his motor vehicle business when he located a housing area off of Interstate 75 and stopped for lunch. He admitted that he was window peeping at three locations and then, according to Griffith, "I had sex with a couple of women after I surprised them by walking into their homes."

Fifteen years after his conviction, Griffith still minimized his actions and deflected responsibility for what he had done. Griffith admitted to cutting telephone lines, and ordering his victims to take off their clothes and not make any noise. He said he never harmed any of his victims nor was he ever armed. He said he never tied them up or used a gag.

After the attacks in Miami County, Griffith told Miami County detectives that he was treated for his sexual addiction problem in Summit County and felt a great deal of remorse and extreme guilt. He said he was convicted for one rape and one burglary. While locked up, he said he was approached by officials from Portage County who accused him of rape. Griffith denied that rape, but said he was convicted of it anyway.

Griffith ended this interview by mentioning that after the Portage County conviction his family visited him and asked if he had committed those attacks. He admitted to his family that he had committed all of them. He said he was glad he was caught. He added that he had no idea how many rapes he had actually committed, but said they were all in Ohio.

Dennis Barr, the criminal division chief of the Stark County prosecutor's office in 2009, was among the first to advise the Ohio Parole Board of his feelings concerning the Griffith case. He wrote:

Please be advised that due to the heinous nature of his crime(s) and his past record this office continues to strongly object to any consideration of early release for the above referenced inmate [William E. Griffith Jr.]. This individual terrorized an entire county by his conduct. This office firmly believes he is a serial rapist and should not be given any consideration for early release.

Philip Paar, the Jackson Township police chief for all but six years of his 25 years with the department, which overlapped the rapes associated with William E. Griffith Jr., retired in 2002 with 30 years of service in local law enforcement. He now is a labor relations officer with the Ohio Department of Youth Services.

Paar said he remembered that Tim Swanson, the county detective, said in the mid-1980's that "there were three suspects, but the best was Bill Griffith." What Paar remembered most vividly was "the panic that gripped the Jackson-Plain Township area."

Asked to classify Griffith after the conviction, Paar said: "He suffers from whatever mental illness rapists suffer from. He was pretty articulate, made a nice impression and showed good demeanor when we talked to him." Questioned further, the Chief said, "I think any kind of behavior like this is dangerous to him and to others. This 'occupation' could have gotten him killed and it almost did at least once." Paar was referring to when Griffith was shot in Akron as a peeping tom suspect.

Focusing on rapists in general, Paar commented that "rapists are about the lowest of the low. They victimize people who aren't in a position to defend themselves. The crime is so horrific that it affects not just the victims but the whole community at large."

Paar said Griffith "certainly was a notorious criminal. He was adept at leading two lives at the same time – father and husband on one hand and serial rapist on the other." Paar added, "I think Chris (Detective Rudy) and those with whom he was working did an outstanding job. Without the work Detective Rudy did, none of those cases would have been solved."

Because of the rapes in Northeast Ohio in the late 1970's and 1980's that could not be prosecuted due to the six-year statute of limitations for sexual assault, then State Representative David Johnson of North Canton sponsored a bill to double the statute of limitations for rape cases to 12 years. Despite pleas from law enforcement officers across the state to increase the statute, the bill died in committee in 1989. However, in 2000, the state legislature increased the statute of limitations to 20 years, which benefits detectives handling cold cases. Along with the advantages of DNA and AFIS processing, victims will now be able to see their attackers brought to trial over two decades after the horrifying incident.

Criminal investigations still demand that detectives have to actively work the case, even with the availability of DNA and AFIS technology. A positive confirmation from fingerprints or DNA identification does not end the work of detectives. Many times it signals the beginning of their work.

Latent prints place the suspect at the scene and can be valuable evidence; however, the detective must provide more information to the prosecutor, who wants to know why the suspect was at the scene. If the suspect had reason to be at the location, then the value of the evidence is probably diminished. DNA also requires further follow up in most cases, even with the crime of rape. The suspect could still claim consent. If an individual had reason to be at the location where DNA was found, prosecution may be hindered.

Technology has made tremendous gains since this case in 1988 and will continue to do so in the future. However, the work of the detective in performing additional follow-up to solidify and bolster evidence will always be necessary. If attention to detail (fingerprint evidence) was paid in this case in the early stages, when Bill Griffith was identified as one of three suspects, it may have been solved years before 1988 and spared numerous victims their suffering.

From 1980-1988 Stark, Summit, Portage and Miami counties alone had 40 reported rapes with the modus operandi of Bill Griffith. The M.O. went hand in hand with the power reassurance typology created by the Behavioral Science Unit of the FBI. As is true with most rapists, the typology reflects a psychological dynamic of aggression in the form of hostility combined with sexuality. The power reassurance rapist is the most common of stranger to stranger rapist. They are organized in their attacks and become increasingly so, as they gain experience. We saw that with Bill as each year passed (i.e.) creating escape routes prior to actually attacking his victims and weeks of planning to pick a victim.

This type of rapist also contains characteristics in attacks that reveal premeditation and planning; voyeuristic activity; weapons predominantly used (i.e.) a knife or gun. The victim is assaulted in her home and is highly vulnerable, with small children also present.

The rapist typically instructs the victim to disrobe and desires foreplay in an attempt to stimulate the victim. The assaults are usually over quickly, and the most common dysfunction reported is erectile incompetence. It would appear that the originators of this typology could have used Bill Griffith as a model.

The rapes that occurred in the four listed Ohio counties from 1980-1988 are all believed to have been perpetrated by Bill Griffith. We know with scientific certainty, (fingerprints and/or DNA), that Bill is guilty of two attacks in 1980, two in 1986 and two in 1988. Through deals made with Bill for no additional prison time in exchange for clearing cases, he admitted to two additional cases in 1986 and two in 1987.

My feeling has always been, if he did the first rapes in 1980, the middle ones in 1986 and the last ones in 1988, it only stands to reason he did ALL of them. Since his arrest and subsequent incarceration, the affected counties have had no other reported rapes with the M.O. listed in this book. Over the years of his incarceration Griffith has told people in the criminal justice system that he has no idea how many women he raped.

Based on my professional experience and research on this topic, Bill Griffith has lied again. I believe he knows exactly how many women he has raped, where they lived and nuances of each attack. I am sure he has relived each rape many times in his private thoughts while locked in an Ohio prison for the last 23 years.

Bill Griffith is as evil as the night is dark. Despicable!

*"We want to see to it that he doesn't leave that institution
unless it's in a bag or in a box."*

Detective Christopher Rudy, Jackson Township Police Department
Akron Beacon Journal, November 2, 1995

Epilogue

In my humble opinion, William E. Griffith Jr. is the
most dangerous criminal ever encountered in Stark County,
Ohio. The pages herein chronicle his crime spree of rape from
1980 through 1988 that caused more devastation than anyone
could imagine.

I am not contending that "my" criminal is worse than
all others. I understand that the taking of a human life is
considered the ultimate crime in our society. Northeast Ohio
has had infamous serial killers or mass murderers, such as
Jeffrey Dahmer (Akron), James Huberty (Massillon), Thomas
Dillon (Canton) and Anthony Sowell (Cleveland). These
monsters committed unspeakable acts and their victims
suffered and died. The families of the victims will mourn their
losses forever. I am not minimizing the loss of these families.

Consider an analogy between divorce and its emotions
and the victim of rape and her emotions. In a divorce, one
spouse often has contact with and sees the other spouse
around town or they are connected through the children from
the marriage. For many people, this can cause a lot of
heartache and rip open old wounds. It can be difficult to
move on. Rape victims (as opposed to murder victims) relive
their nightmares many times over. The court process,
counseling, parole hearings, certain settings, the time of year
and even *AN ODOR* triggers a wave of emotion.

But when you bury a loved one, be it from murder, an accident or from natural means, there is a sense of closure. There is a feeling that he or she is gone, in a better place, and that they are now safe. You mourn their loss; however, there is finality in these situations. I submit that the rapist – the violent sexual predator – leaves more damage and devastation behind than the serial killer or multiple murderers. He touches and wrecks more lives than the killer.

When anyone looks at the destruction that William E. Griffith Jr. caused over many years, it gives one pause. This story alluded to 60 plus incidents that mirror the activities to which William E. Griffith Jr. pled guilty. Attach just one victim with each incident. That totals 60 victims touched by Griffith's violent sexual appetite.

According to the Bureau of Justice Statistics, which produces statistics from the FBI's Uniform Crime Reports (UCR) and the National Crime Victimization Survey (NCVS), less than _half_ of all completed acts of rape are reported. Bearing that fact in mind, I can say with reasonable certainty that there are an additional 60 victims and incidents that can be attributed to William E. Griffith Jr. That is a total of 120 victims. We all know, however, that the families of the victims also are touched by what occurred. So, I can say with a high degree of probability that there are, at a minimum, at least three other people (spouse, parent, and child) affected per victim.

Using that formula, 120 victims plus 360 indirect victims total 480 people who were touched by the violent sexual acts of William E. Griffith Jr. Moreover, his five children, their children and his ex-wives are victims, too. I can safely estimate there are 500 people who have been affected by and had their lives altered in some fashion because of this one, violent sexual predator. Unbelievable!

The infamous Northeast Ohio killers I listed above may each have six to 20 victims. The crime of murder has a 100 percent report rate with UCR, and the NCVS does not come into play for obvious reasons. I am not attempting to minimize the horror the killer committed and the loss to the family members of these victims. But I believe the violent sexual predator should receive more attention. Violent sexual predators should be dealt with more severely and kept out of society.

Regardless of how you obtain the news, whatever news media you choose, every couple of days, weeks or months, there is a report of a child disappearance or a female abduction. No trace of the victim can be found. Everyone is riveted by the suspense until the case is resolved. Far too often, the result is tragic. Even one tragic result is one too many.

For example, in February 2010 the nation heard the story of John Albert Gardner III, who had raped and killed 17-year-old Chelsea King of Poway, California. In March 2010, Gardner was tied to the rape and murder of 14-year-old Amber Dubois, who had gone missing in February 2009 near Escondido High School, which is 10 miles north of the location where Chelsea King vanished. From January 2008 to January 2010, Gardner was a registered sex offender in Escondido, a suburb of San Diego. He had served five years of a six-year prison sentence for molesting a 13-year-old neighbor girl in San Diego in 2000. He completed parole in 2008.

In February 2010, the nation also learned that in 1991 Philip Garrido had kidnapped Jaycee Dugard. For the next 18 years, he and his wife, Nancy, held Jaycee captive as their sex slave in the backyard of their Antioch, California, home.

In March 2010, we watched and learned as authorities in North Dakota announced they were hunting for a "high risk sex offender" who had cut off his GPS monitoring device. Thomas Jose Eppler, 24, was described as a lifetime sexual-offender registrant with a criminal history in Minnesota and Iowa. Police had no idea if he was still in the Fargo area or had fled the state. However, police knew Eppler had an alias (Jose Munoz Gutierrez) and had been convicted of sexually assaulting a female acquaintance in North Dakota.

In April 2010, police in Kansas City, Missouri, charged Bernard Jackson with raping five women in the Kansas City neighborhood of Waldo from September 2009 through February 2010. Jackson had been charged in the 1980's with raping four other women in the Kansas City area.

In July 2010, Tushon Brown of East Liberty, Pennsylvania, sexually mutilated and killed 14-year old Lauren Dies, who had refused to have sex with him for $200. Brown had been in prison in Pennsylvania since 2002 after he pled guilty to charges of rape, sexually deviate intercourse, aggravated assault and the burglary of a woman in July 2001. Two months prior to that attack, Brown had raped another woman at knifepoint in the same apartment building. Brown and his two earlier victims all had attended the same college in downtown Pittsburgh. They all lived in the same apartment building. Brown had received a sentence of seven to 15 years. After serving seven years and five months, Brown was paroled by the Pennsylvania Board of Probation and Parole. It only took him seven months to reoffend!

Aside from immediate family members, an investigation always begins with a check of all known registered sex offenders in a 1-, 2-, 5- or 10-mile radius. I know. I've done it. Only a minor number of investigations derive a suspect from that group. Most people believe a suspect is always derived from known registered offenders; however, it is only a small number of cases when that actually happens. My recommendation is that the violent sexual predator/sexual psychopath (or however a state classifies its sexual offenders (*e.g.*, Tier I, Tier II or Tier III), should never again be assimilated into society. Period. End of discussion. I am only referring to the worst offenders at the top of the state's categorized system (i.e., violent sexual predator, sexual psychopath or Tier 3 offender). The lower-level sex offenders can continue to be dealt with and receive treatment, as states see fit. What I propose is only for the category of the worst sex offender.

The death penalty is extremely controversial; however, it does impact recidivism. I am not that extreme. I suggest that a form of civil commitment be authorized in every state in the country. In July 2006, Congress adopted the Adam Walsh Act (AWA) as federal law. The AWA provides for civil commitment at the federal level.

In a nutshell, civil commitment is a civil process that assesses the likelihood that an inmate would reoffend or still poses a threat to society. This is done at the expiration of his or her prison sentence. The former prisoner is placed in an institutional setting or hospital-like setting for his or her remaining days. Annual assessments are required, but the former prisoner remains out of society.

Civil commitment does not guarantee offenders will always be committed. However, the possibility of release back into society is greatly diminished. It is a far superior system for protecting the public than the state system that does not provide for civil commitment. My personal belief is that the violent sexual predator/sexual psychopath should never be released. Currently, there are 20 states that have civil commitment laws similar to the AWA.

Ohio adopted the Adam Walsh Act in 2007 to comply with federal regulations streamlining sex offender registration and the computerized tracking system. The program known as ESORN classifies sex offenders in the three tiered system with Tier I offenders being the least dangerous and Tier III the most serious offenders. The hope is to have a streamlined system across the country. As of the writing of this book, only Ohio and Delaware have adopted the Adam Walsh Act. The federal government has given the remaining states waivers about complying with the AWA with a warning they will not be eligible for federal criminal justice funds unless they enact the legislation.

My fear is that the Adam Walsh Act will suffer the same fate as the motor voter registration law enacted in 1993. Subsequent enforcement of the motor voter registration law has never been a priority for the states and languishes to this day.

Ohio has yet to enact the civil commitment component of the AWA legislation due to cost constraints. However, the AWA does provide federal grants to assist states in implementation, including the housing and treatment of offenders.

Every state should provide a civil commitment process for its most serious sexual offenders. Our wives, mothers and children deserve nothing less than to be protected from these monsters. William E. Griffith Jr. has not been granted parole thus far, and should **_NEVER_** be released! I hope that Griffith's deeds chronicled in The Last Victim provide the impetus for a change in legislation so such events never happen again.

At the time of publication Bill Griffith was 69 years old. When he has completed his definite sentence he will be 96 years old.

About the Authors

Lawman-turned-author Christopher Rudy has been a law enforcement officer over 30 years, with more than half that time involved in criminal investigation. Now with a major security company, he maintains his law enforcement commission through the Summit County, Ohio Sheriff's Office. The highly decorated civil servant holds degrees in Organizational Management and Criminal Justice. The father of two grown children, Rudy has received countless hours of training in all aspects of criminal investigation, including graduating in the 196th session of the FBI National Academy in Quantico, Virginia. He also is a veteran of the United States Air Force.

Police and Fire reporter/editor George Davis spent 42 years in the newspaper business before retiring from the Akron Beacon Journal six weeks before 9-11. Six weeks later, he became the city of Canton's first and only Public Information Officer as liaison between city agencies and safety forces and regional news media. In 2009, the father of five children teamed with long-time friend Rudy to assist with this book, tracing major events of one of the most intriguing and disturbing crime sagas spanning three decades.

CPSIA information can be obtained at www.ICGtesting.com
Printed in the USA
BVOW011149261012

304050BV00004B/6/P

9 781468 017601